PENGUIN MODERN CLASSICS
Fourteen Years with Boss

ASHOKAMITRAN, born in 1931 in Secunderabad, is one of the most distinguished contemporary Indian writers. In a prolific career that began in 1955, he has written over 250 short stories along with two dozen novels and novellas, in addition to a steady output of columns, essays and book reviews, earning him a central place in post-Independence Tamil literature. His work has been translated into many Indian and European languages. Five major novels as well as four collections of short fiction from his oeuvre are available in English translation. His years of rich and diverse contribution to Tamil literature have brought him many honours, including the Sahitya Akademi Award (1996). Ashokamitran lives and works in Chennai.

ASHOKAMITRAN

Fourteen Years with Boss

PENGUIN BOOKS

An imprint of Penguin Random House

PENGUIN BOOKS

USA | Canada | UK | Ireland | Australia
New Zealand | India | South Africa | China | Singapore

Penguin Books is part of the Penguin Random House group of companies
whose addresses can be found at global.penguinrandomhouse.com

Published by Penguin Random House India Pvt. Ltd
4th Floor, Capital Tower 1, MG Road,
Gurugram 122 002, Haryana, India

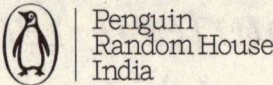

First published by Penguin Books India 2016

Copyright © Ashokamitran 2016

10 9 8 7 6 5 4 3 2

The views and opinions expressed in this book are the author's own and
the facts are as reported by him which have been verified to the extent
possible, and the publishers are not in any way liable for the same.

ISBN 9780143423294

Typeset in Dante MT Std by Manipal Digital Systems, Manipal

Printed at Repro India Limited

www.penguin.co.in

MIX
Paper from
responsible sources
FSC® C047271

This is a legitimate digitally printed version of the book and therefore might not
have certain extra finishing on the cover.

Contents

Contents

Introduction

I was twenty when I came across an issue of the *Illustrated Weekly of India* containing, among a bunch of sterling reading material, an article titled 'The Great Dream Bazaar' by Ashokamitran. It was actually the first of a series of articles and at that time not only those in Tamil Nadu but readers in other parts of India as well keenly looked forward to successive instalments. The articles contained a pleasantly unpredictable sequence of events and details (like an English poet in a Madras studio). Of course, at that time I did not discern the artistic and stylistic aspects of the pieces but my friends, relatives and I were excited that what we knew about films hazily and what we did not know at all, was issuing out of the articles in an exceedingly informative and entertaining manner.

It was the year 1984 and Tamil Nadu had outgrown the MGR–Sivaji Ganesan syndrome and was gradually settling down to another pair, Kamalahasan–Rajinikanth. Kamal Hasaan was Kamalahasan in those days. In the north, Rajesh Khanna had given way to the tall phenomenon called Amitabh Bachchan. A film society movement was flourishing in Madras and though my generation listened to Ilayaraja's film songs and watched Kamalahasan's films, we worshipped Kurosawa and Fellini. A separate genre of films known as the art film had come about with its votaries in Aravindan, Ritwik Ghatak, Kumar Shahani and Mani Kaul. There was the middle cinema, or the parallel cinema, headed by Basu Bhattacharya, Shyam Benegal and others. Satyajit Ray had created his great *Charulata* and Sippy's *Sholay* was still drawing crowds. In such an atmosphere of abundance and variety, 'The Great Dream Bazaar' (which

I knew was the editor's title and that the writer had called it 'My Years with Boss') made reflecting on Indian films and movie business an intellectual pursuit. The films themselves may not be imposingly great but the panorama of the entire film movement in the context of prevailing sociological, political and cultural forces of India made them a challenging and highly rewarding field of study. The articles also made one more tolerant towards popular cinema. There must be a tiny bit of truth to make hundreds of thousands of filmgoers spend their hard-earned money and sit through the film in a dark, uncomfortable hall for three hours. When that tiny bit of truth is out of sync, the film is rejected mercilessly.

In the Upanishads there is a discussion between a guru and his disciple about a particular daily ritual. The guru had said that the ritual performed three times a day was valueless as far as mukti, or freedom, was concerned but still had to be performed. Naturally, the disciple asks why. The guru replied that at least while performing the ritual one is protected from accumulating harmful karma. The history of films is now important not only to film scholars but to all thinking men and women with a concern for people and society. Many histories are straightforward narratives of events in sequence. Very often mere chronology leaves one unconvinced. But if the historian is able to capture the life and breath of events and make us believe that those men and women really existed, then history becomes meaningful. It is this liveliness and vivacity that makes *Fourteen Years with Boss* a brief but special book of history.

In Ashokamitran's fiction, human beings are written about as human beings with all their failings and shortcomings but still presented with dignity and earnestness. This book is vintage Ashokamitran. In the growing body of literature on Indian films, *Fourteen Years with Boss* is sure to find a choice place.

Hyderabad,   T. RAVISHANKAR
15 July 2010

1

My Father's Friend

A hundred years ago, in the Nizam's Hyderabad, people built palaces even if it was a single-room house. However small the actual living place was, the 'palace' had a wide patio and a broad veranda in the front. The veranda was where guests were received; street vendors lowered their baskets to help the resident pick and choose vegetables and fruits, ice cream was bought and eaten, newspapers browsed, and overnight guests accommodated with pillows and blankets to sleep off the night. Percy's Hotel, considered the best in Secunderabad, in 1940, couldn't help but look like a palace. With not much room in the front, there was a portico and broad verandas on all four sides. Tall, thin pillars delicately connected at the top by thin arches. Tall doors and a very high ceiling. The residents were provided with a table fan, table light and cot with a mosquito net. The view from the front rooms was enchanting. One saw the racecourse which had an exquisite pavilion. There were very few vehicles in the city so the hotel did not need much parking space. If one had keen eyes he could see the resident in the room, which was not too far from the road, Alexandria Road in this case. It was in one such room in Percy's that I first saw the Boss along with my father.

S.S. Vasan, the Boss, had been a kind of salesman right from his teens. He sold small booklets and timetables. After a while he wrote books himself which he sold without claiming to be an author. He produced a truly voluminous book called *500 Ways to Start Small Businesses*. I do not know how many put his lessons to practice but the book had no second edition and so no one could trace the author if anything went wrong or right. Then he wrote another voluminous book titled *Kudumba Vinotha Kathaikal* (strange stories that have happened within the family). He had a postbox and started a mail-order business selling bits of inexpensive but attractive articles, like a pistol which did not require a licence, hand-held spring articles for self-defence, etc. And he would send them with a box of pins with a claim that a thousand articles had been shipped for a rupee. When a tottering monthly magazine came his way, he bought it with all the money he had— about three hundred rupees. Since he was himself a writer, he managed to get a band of talented but unpublished writers and embarked on journalism with all the enthusiasm possible. He made the magazine a totally error-free compilation of short pieces of various kinds— fiction, reportage, current affairs, parodies, pen portraits and jokes. It will appear now that Ronald Ross of the *New Yorker* took ideas from Vasan to start his weekly. Vasan knew his readership was from the neo-literates and so kept things simple and straightforward but dealt with a range of subjects from movies to book reviews, metaphysics to motoring.

Vasan's early life was filled with pain. He lost his father early and his mother worked to the bone from morning to evening to feed the boy and educate him. She had him finish school and even managed to put him in college when he said he could no longer bear to see his mother slave to make a man out of him. He abandoned college and took on a mail-order business and also worked as an advertising agent. He was extremely scrupulous in his transactions. This integrity lasted all through his life and he was never short of customers although he did suffer a few setbacks. When a film studio came up for auction, he bought it for a few thousand rupees and transformed it to symbolize wholesome entertainment.

For this, he needed not only writers but also dependable technicians.

So, how did horses come into his life, why and how? No one had answers. He rarely talked about his racing days but it is certain he was soon considered a specialist in the choice of horses and in betting in individual events. Secunderabad at the beginning of World War II was an important racing town. How and where he had sent word to my father, I do not know. But my father took me along when he went to see Vasan.

How did my father and Vasan get to be close? This I learnt from my father. It appears that when Vasan had a bookshop, my father went and selected a few books but he was short of cash to buy all of them. Could not be much— probably less than ten rupees—but those were days when credit was possible only to dealers and not to members of the public. My father returned a few books but Vasan said, 'You could send the money once you reach Secunderabad.'

'What if I didn't?'

'You are not the type.'

That is how it started. For some time, Vasan tried to make my father his agent for his magazine but my father declined. But both continued to be in touch and when Vasan married off his daughter in 1950, my father was an honoured guest.

Vasan became a truly big film producer in 1943 with an extraordinary film called *Mangamma Sabatham*. The film was set in a period that could either be seventeenth or eighteenth century when there were petty kings and chieftains. It is in this film that Vasan revealed a flair for making very effective use of a smattering of sounds which sounded like a language when actually no such thing existed. The heroine played a gypsy and seduced the prince who had forcefully married her only to imprison her for life. The film was a great hit in spite of the fear of bombardment by the Japanese. There was even a threat of invasion.

Vasan made his studio a model studio, and people from far and wide were curious to come and see Gemini Studios (in fact, the outfit had three studios). He knew that not only an army but any large group of people working in a confined area would need a timely and sumptuous feed. The Gemini mess, or canteen, was just as famous as the studio.

It is possible that it was at that point in his career that I saw him in Percy Hotel along with my father. It is likely that he was then in the process of quitting the races.

I would also like to divulge another important fact here. These introductory lines have been written exactly thirty years after the chapters that follow, which make a volume of *Fourteen Years with Boss*.

Chennai,   Ashokamitran
2015

2

A Walk to the Hospital

January 4, 1951. At around eight in the morning, my father said to me, 'Come, let's go to the hospital.' This hospital visit was not out of choice. It was because of Dr D'Souza.

The Chilkalguda Railway Dispensary had two doctors and two pharmacists. The two doctors were Dr Singaperumal and Dr D'Souza. I do not think they were more than licentiates. Sixty years ago, one could do a licentiate course in medicine and call himself a doctor. I have no doubt both were very good doctors. They could look into the throat, feel the pulse and know what was wrong with the patient.

There was another course named LM&S—licentiate in medicine and surgery. People who got this licence could perform surgery up to a point. Major surgery needed an MBBS. Secunderabad did not have many of this kind. People travelled to Hyderabad, Poona or Madras for major surgeries.

The Chilkalguda dispensary always had patients waiting. There were verandas on either side of the consulting room. The left was for women and the right for men. My father always went by the right veranda and in the consulting room, would pull up a chair for himself. This was all right for Singaperumal who made house visits but I am now sure D'Souza didn't like it. He was very cold to my father and to all of us. All that the dispensary gave was a 'mixture' called Carminative mixture and magsulph. Magnesium sulphate is a purgative now not used at all. But in the 1940s, it was a kind of cure-all medicine. It must be admitted that in those days, the main cause of illness was poor toilet habits. I studied in a school with a thousand other students and all we had were two water taps and four urinals. We drank water straight from the tap and in all my six years at the school, there was no case of water infection. I do not think that father had any infection. He was just not feeling well. He did go to Chilkalguda a few times but the Railway rules needed the patient to go to Lalaguda if two days of the Carminative mixture did not cure the patient. So we walked.

At the Lalaguda hospital, father needed a fresh prescription sheet. The doctor on duty first felt father's pulse. I didn't understand what he told my father. Then he placed his stethoscope on my father's chest and said, 'Better get admitted straightaway.'

We came out of the consultation room. The hospital was a sprawling, tall, tiled single-storeyed building. The British had indeed run a very big military establishment and when the first World War was over, they gave all their barracks and buildings to the Nizam's

Railway. The hospital resembled a quarters and the quarters resembled the offices which in turn resembled the bungalows allotted to the English officers of the Railway.

My father said, 'I will give you my coat and cap. Bring my lunch before ten thirty. The medical officer will come to my bed at eleven.'

I went home and told my mother about father's lunch. She was surprised. Father was not in the best of health but did he need hospitalization? He went to Lalaguda because D'Souza was not authorized to advise leave of absence for more than two days. Further, he had written in my father's medical case sheet that the patient was treatable only in a hospital. Our designated hospital was the Railway Hospital at Lalaguda.

My mother was worried. 'Last night also he needed rice bran fomentation.' This fomentation applied on the chest and on the back was supposed to loosen up the congestion in the lungs.

My father was in his early fifties and I have heard that when he was young he was a wrestler. Wrestling is an unusual pursuit for a Brahmin and when he was admitted in the Lalaguda hospital, his biceps seemed that of an athlete, not of a clerk in the Railway office. It was my mother who needed hospitalization on a number of occasions, and once, she was supposed to have needed extensive treatment for double pneumonia. At the time, Father would not only go to the hospital every day but he would also cook food for us and make each meal a special one by frying Malabar papad. Normal South Indian *appalam* could be made edible by directly roasting over fire but Malabar papad had to be deep fried.

I brought his lunch at ten thirty. But the medical officer was already at my father's bedside. He was a Reddy, a community very influential in those parts. Instead of living off miles of well-irrigated land, this Reddy had chosen to go to England and become a doctor of medicine. Maybe he understood the local people and their ailments better but the hospital had a chief medical officer who was an Englishman. Once, when my father was away, my younger brother had jumped off a running bus and at Chilkalguda they said that I should take him to Lalaguda to see the chief medical officer. I had to look up to talk to him—he was about seven feet tall. I think he asked me what made my brother jump off a bus. I could not think of any satisfactory answer. I had to see the chief medical officer once again, when my tonsils had to be removed. They starved me for a whole day, gave me magnesium sulphate, and not satisfied I had an empty stomach, administered a humiliating enema. Before all this, for a whole month, I had to take a 10-cc injection every third day to help my blood to coagulate. The chief medical officer removed my tonsils, or so everyone thought. He had left a tiny lump that in a matter of a fortnight grew to its full size. I am sure he felt sorry but we couldn't go through another surgery. Even today, I function with only half of my throat cleared of tonsils. I fell ill many times after the surgery but the Railway doctors never mentioned that my cold or fever was due to my tonsils, which was like a pyramid of flesh laid on one of its sides.

For a whole week, I carried Father's morning coffee and around ten his lunch, and in the evening, my mother carried a simple meal for him. There seemed to be nothing alarming about my father's condition. The doctors could have been a little more communicative but there was no compulsion in those days for doctors to explain what was wrong with the patient. I was too inexperienced and it never struck me that I should know the cause of my father's hospitalization.

My father had walked nearly a mile and a half to the hospital but in a week's time, he began to look like a patient. He dozed most of the time helplessly and almost stopped talking.

The fourteenth of January is usually celebrated as Pongal for Tamils and Sankranthi for Telugus. Secunderabad and Lalaguda, Malkajgiri, Ramakrishnapuram were all Telugu areas. If father had been at home, he and I would have gone to the Monda market a day before and brought home a whole sugar cane together with its roots and crowning leaves, and on Pongal, he would perform a ritual worshipping the sun in the open. I got sugar cane and some fruit this time, and mother did the puja she knew, and afterwards, I took some Pongal to my father. He didn't seem to be interested in eating. A day prior to Pongal, that is the thirteenth of January, a junior doctor had told me, 'Inform your people,' and went away. What was I to inform and to whom? My father had a brother and a cousin living in Secunderabad and they already knew he was in the hospital. For people at that time, a hospital was a place where sick people healed. My mother had been in a hospital half a dozen times, my father had been in the two hospitals of Secunderabad and I had also been in Lalaguda hospital, though in a different ward. I went and told my mother, and she couldn't understand either. When I went to my uncle's house and told him what the junior doctor had said, no one reacted. But my uncle's son-in-law said, 'You are very bold people.'

Again, I couldn't make out what he meant. I went to the hospital around 8 p.m. My mother was wailing. My father had died at 7.45.

3

Home We Brought Him Dead

I went in search of the doctor on duty. As a matter of fact, no medical personnel had come to examine my father the whole day of fourteenth January. Patients and medical emergencies don't have holidays. There was no indication from any of them that my father was dying. Death was the last thing on our minds. Father had been in a semi-conscious state on a number of occasions before but had revived after a sip of coffee or tea. I was too young and inexperienced to interpret a doctor saying, 'Tell your relatives.'

A doctor was sighted at around 8.15. I asked him, 'What happened to my father?'

He evaded answering me. He took out a writing pad which was actually a pad of blank death certificates. He wrote down my father's name, the day he was admitted and the day of discharge. In that blank page he wrote, 'Died due to heart failure.' He signed and tore off the sheet from the pad and gave it to me. 'You should vacate the bed by 9 p.m.' he said.

'How do I take him home?'

'No tongawallah will take a dead body. Better a bullock cart.'

'Where will I find one?'

'I have no idea. But you might get one near the railway station.'

'Where is the railway station?'

The doctor first shouted one name. Then another. Then a third. A person appeared. The doctor said to him, '*Inko rayilway station kahan hai batao.*'

He told me, 'Tell the bullockcart man that it is a dead body.'

By the time I got a bullock cart to the hospital they had covered my father's face. My mother was yet to realize that she was now a widow.

The cart man and I carried the body and placed it in the cart. I asked my mother to get into the cart and hold the head. Though the body had gone stiff, the head swayed. It was a slow, long walk, quite in contrast to the walk my father and I had just ten days ago.

Whether the funeral rites carried the dead man's soul to a restful place and also ensured the survivors of an honourable place in the hereafter, they certainly had a way of preventing the family from wallowing in the loss. It was the hour of the priests. They took over the house for the next six hours, at the end of which I led the funeral procession carrying a pot containing pieces of glowing twigs that I had lighted myself at the beginning of the

Ashokamitran

religious rites. I was expected not to look back.
I could feel a large number of people following
me. My father had lived a little over thirty years
in the town of Secunderabad and had known
just about half the town's people. He spoke
their language, listened to their accounts of
joy and sorrow, gains and losses. He brimmed
with calm and contentment until the marriage
of his eldest daughter. The second daughter's
marriage increased the lines on his forehead.
In less than three years, he had me leading his
funeral procession.

Two days later, we received a condolence
note from the general manager—J.N. Nanda—
the first and the last Indian general manager of the
Nizam's State Railway. Soon Nizam's Railway
was to be integrated into South Central Railway
with the office of the head at Nagpur. So no more
Nizam's Railway. My father, if he had been alive,
would have been transferred to Nagpur.

The condolence letter was followed by an
officious letter—a kind of notice one could call

it. We were expected to vacate the quarters in two weeks.

Vacate the house and go elsewhere! We had become so integrated with the barracks that we couldn't imagine ourselves in a different setting. Our quarters had large rooms and my father saw to it that no inch of the house remained unused. Four huge tables; a dozen large wooden chairs; three wooden cots and a cast-iron bed that could be dismantled; mattresses for all the beds and over a dozen pillows; a large wooden cradle with a strong stand to allow for it to be rocked. The cradle had seen a dozen babies. Now that none of us were babies, we sat in it when it contained no clothes to be washed by a washerman. There were dozens of group photographs with his brothers, living and dead, and his colleagues; a large painting of his first son who died at the age of fourteen. Also a victim of medical miscalculation and callousness; and a hundred pictures of gods and goddesses of the Hindu pantheon; the best of

Raja Ravi Varma's pictures cut from the ICI calendars and framed. Two gramophones and more than 200 78-rpm records which had given us many hours of enjoyment. We had many sets, which were a set of four or five or six records containing a whole drama with a number of songs. Our favourite was *Alli Arjuna*, a musical drama with Abdul Khader, quite famous in the 1930s for his rendering of spoken and sung Tamil. He played Arjuna in *Alli Arjuna*, and Kovalan in *Kovalan*. They were called drama sets and five or six companies always worked on creating new records or organizing new drama sets. Each company had its own players and there was a company called Saraswathi Stores that led all the rest. I believe the recording and 'cutting' of the wax records were done in Dacca, Bengal. The drama troupe was always a compact one and since it was all audio, one player played more than one role. A whole play in gramophone records, even after movies came on in a big way. We had some rare records (also called discs) and one such carried an election speech by Indian National Congress leader S. Satyamurthy. In three minutes he rendered an extremely effective election propaganda speech. The other side contained a song by a veteran singer rendering an election propaganda song as though it were a classical song. Now the time had come to decide whether we could cling to all our possessions that filled the large Railway house. My father did buy a lot of things not necessarily useful to anyone else.

I took loads of wooden furniture and the gramophones and records to an auction and got just a little less than a hundred rupees. We gave away most of the pictures. The group photographs, all excellent examples of quality plate photographs, put us in a dilemma. But our big worry was the cow and the three calves.

Rearing cattle was the last thing we were qualified for. There was a certain joy in complaining about the ever-late milkman. But one day, he brought a buffalo and tied it to the gate of our house. Obviously, my father had lent him a few rupees—fifty at the most—and he thought giving away a buffalo was the best way to punish us while seeming to repay the loan. But in a matter of months, it seemed impossible to live without a cow or a buffalo. The Railway quarters wouldn't mind even if we reared an elephant. In fact, keeping an animal, even cows and buffaloes, needed a licence from the cantonment authorities. The form you needed to fill to get a licence to keep a pet at home started with an elephant and ended with pigeons.

Now it seems a miracle, but in 1951, I managed all this and left the Railway quarters, moved to one place, then another, until finally moving into a modest house on the outskirts of the city. I couldn't feel more grateful to my two friends, M.K. Sundarkumar and his brother, M.K. Selvakumar. Their father, my school principal, Prof. M.S. Kotiswaran, was the guardian angel of our family.

Our final address in Secunderabad was 'So-and-so, near Durgabai House, Begumpet'. I hadn't seen Durgabai or any of her people but she allowed our cow and the three calves to graze in the spacious compound in which her bungalow stood. I started on my bicycle at six in the morning and went to a house in Hyderabad to coach two students. I then went to teach in a coaching school. It would be a little after noon. I would bicycle to lower Tank Bund and go to a farm. I would be there not too early and not later than quarter to one. For half a rupee, the farm sold a large, luxuriously grown long grass called guinea grass. With the grass firmly tied to my luggage carrier, I would take a shortcut to go to Begumpet along the cantonment slum houses of Mettugadda. After lunch I went to a school hostel to oversee the accounts, and in the evening, coach another high school student. All this was possible because of Prof. Kotiswaran. Life went on quietly, our family was more than satisfied, we had a good friend in the postman who took me to the rationing office and got cards for us, two non-existing aunts and two dogs. The Hyderabad state under the Nizam was generous in the issuance of ration cards. All you got as rations was maize and, occasionally, sugar. As a matter of fact, we should have got sugar generously because the Nizam's state had a sugar factory. But from 1939 onwards, the sugar we got each month could be carried in a shirt pocket.

One day, the postman brought me a fancy looking envelope. That letter changed my destiny.

4

The Boss Decides

The letter was from S.S. Vasan. He was the boss of Gemini Studios, editor–publisher of *Ananda Vikatan*, the most popular and influential Tamil weekly magazine of the times and also the owner of an extremely prestigious film distribution unit. It was he that my father and I met at Percy's Hotel when I was about nine or ten years old.

The letter was handwritten. Vasan said he was shocked to learn that my father had died prematurely. He said that my father was very close to him, a friend who never expected anything from him. (I understood this line later. Gemini Studios had a number of Vasan's old friends in employment, not at all of any significance to the real task of the studio, namely, making movies. He even gave a nondescript job to an old teacher of his by the name of Poduval. One special thing about Poduval was that V.K. Krishna Menon came to see him one day.) Could I make a trip to Madras in the near future and see him personally?

I do not remember informing Vasan of my father's death. I sent just one telegram to my mother's brother. As I have been repeatedly stating, I was too inexperienced to handle the death of the head of the family and assume the role myself. Those were days of very small salaries and all we got as father's provident fund and gratuity was Rs 15,000. We looked for a house to buy and in fact almost decided to buy one in Sitaphalmandi. A small house with a yard and an exclusive, protected water supply connection. Those were the days of 'dry' latrines. We had the same thing in the Railway quarters too. We should have trusted our instinct instead of listening to an unconcerned person: don't buy Muslim property!

We probably dropped the idea of buying the house also because the Begumpet house was so convenient. Of course, we didn't have electricity but we were quite happy with kerosene lamps. What was I to do with Vasan's invitation? He obviously had something in mind.

I asked Kotiswaran. He said nothing should be rejected offhand.

I dropped a postcard to Vasan saying that I was making a trip to Madras. Those were the days when 90 per cent of postal mail was in the form of postcards. Interview intimations were on printed postcards.

I also informed my uncle that I would be there on the fifteenth of November.

Those were the days of reservation-free travel with few options. A day and a night to reach Madras by two express trains—one had to change trains at Bezwada which years later became Vijayawada

By Indian standards, I was still a boy and could squeeze myself in a railway carriage and feel fit and energetic. I was at Vasan's residence, Gemini House, and was greeted by an elderly man. He was Vasan's maternal uncle. Vasan not only supported a number of his old friends but found jobs for a very large number of relations, near and some not so near. I showed him Vasan's letter. Of course, he had known my father. Wasn't he one of a group of very important guests at Vasan's daughter's wedding a year ago?

Someone brought me a cup of coffee. I hadn't started to drink it when Vasan appeared. He said, 'I have not decided yet. How soon can you move to Madras?'

I didn't understand what he meant. I said, 'Twenty-four hours.'

He smiled realizing that he had not conveyed the whole message. He said, 'I can give you a job. I asked you how long it will take you to wind up your matters and move to Madras.'

'My father died in January. I am performing the monthly ceremonies. The annual ceremony should fall in February next year.'

'You can do one thing. Come to Madras soon after the annual ceremony. You can fix up a house in about a month or two. Then go to Secunderabad and bring your mother and others, and all your things.'

He had decided that I should join one of his companies. He was a short man and wore a dhoti and white shirt but his strength was overpowering because he was a self-made man.

I kept the coffee glass on the chair and was preparing to leave. He said, 'Finish your coffee. Let me get you some money.'

He gave me 100 rupees, twice the amount I had to spend for the trip. I saw *Awara* at Rajakumari and was overcome by the film. Raj Kapoor hadn't lost his innocence. Hindi films were so different from Tamil and Telugu films.

I told my uncle what had happened and left Madras by the following day's Grand Trunk Express.

I told my friends and Prof. Kotiswaran. For him, migrating from one state to another wasn't a big deal. Hadn't he burnt his bridges to become the principal of Mahbub College in a place not many people spelt right the first time? He gave a new face to the school. His predecessor had not taken classes but Professor Kotiswaran took English classes for the final two batches. He organized oratory contests at the class level and also at the school level. He wore the scout dress himself and made the two troops, Five and Forty-nine, come alive. He presided over the meeting when C. Rajagopalachari had parted with Gandhi and the rest on the issue of Pakistan. He presided over musical concerts that took place in Secunderabad. To the horror and delight of thousands of Tamils, he made his school students enact a three-hour play. For a few months, he went to Colombia, Washington D.C., to get a master's degree. He did everything to stir the envy of the upper crust of Secunderabad and had to face their hostility. But adventure was something he didn't shirk from. He told me, 'Go.'

My mother didn't react. When father was alive, she made most decisions. Now she drifted. My younger brother was appearing for his final examination in school. In Madras, I would have to put him in a college. I had a younger sister in the eighth class. I would have to find a suitable school for her. But what appalled me were the things we needed to transport to Madras. A huge teak wooden bureau. Two oversized wooden benches on which my mother slept. A huge table. A sewing machine. A large wooden box containing a selection of books of English literature. My father was only an SSLC, which meant that he never went to college but his collection contained Shakespeare, Byron, Scott, Dickens, Thackeray, Eliot (not T.S.). He had read them all and could recite from memory Shakespeare's *Rape of Lucrece*. He shifted his house a number of times and walked a mile or so to buy vegetables and groceries

For a while, I was excited too. What would my job be like? I will miss the masala dosa of Tajmahal restaurant. I will miss Parade Ground. Husain Sagar lake . . .

When I informed my three students, they were shocked. I believe they started weeping. The parents thought they could retain me by doubling my fees. 'Please stay till April. We will pay you 500 rupees.' It was a problem wrenching myself away from the boys and their parents. If they had told me before that I was so important to them, I would not have responded to Vasan's letter. Destiny.

A week after my father's death anniversary, I went to Madras. Vasan asked me to see him at the studios. He was not happy about a number of things. Would I like to be an inspector of cinema halls and check the number of people in the audience and see if that tallied with collections?

He was not clear what position would be suitable to me. He said, 'Come tomorrow.'

I went the next day. 26 February 1952.

Vasan came to his office around noon. Straightaway he said, 'You will be the assistant to the public relations officer. He will come here now. Meanwhile, go and see the business secretary.'

The business secretary was yet another beneficiary of Vasan's gratitude to the father of the secretary who ran a small eatery where Vasan's mother had worked in order to send Vasan to school.

Obviously, Vasan had already told the PRO, one P.P. Nambiar, that he should put up with a new assistant. Nambiar was at least six feet tall and looked like a police officer. I later learnt that he was an inspector at the Salt and Excise Department in Bezwada, and had been writing letters to Vasan about Vasan's films almost on a daily basis. The punishment Vasan could think of was to offer him a job. Would anyone give up a Central government job? Nambiar had done his master's degree and would have retired as a deputy commissioner if not commissioner of the excise department. Again, destiny.

In three years' time, he was made Vasan's secretary and I became the PRO. Instinctively, I thought just being a staff member of a film studio, however famous and respected, was not sufficient. I began to write. By 1953, I had written half a dozen short stories and had also begun a novel. When the All India Radio announced a competition for a one-hour play, I wrote one and won the second prize. In 1954, I published my first short story in English. When I published my first Tamil story in 1957, I had published half a dozen stories in English in

Bangalore, Bombay, Delhi and Calcutta. The title of the Tamil story is significant: *The Ending of the Play*. It should have been *The Beginning of a New Destiny*.

5

What a Way to Treat a Lady

In *The Rajaji Story 1937–1972* by
Rajmohan Gandhi, on page 243
containing Rajaji's diary jottings for
1953, there is an entry: 'Saw Gemini
Vasan's picture *Avvaiyar . . .*'[1]

After the stunning success of the Tamil film
Samsaram and the even greater success of its
Hindi version, *Sansar*, at Gemini Studios, we
released another *Samsaram*-like film, *The Three*

---

[1] Rajmohan Gandhi, *The Rajaji Story 1937–1972*,
Bombay: Bharatiya Vidya Bhavan, 1984.

Sons, in 1952. In several respects, this latter film was superior to the earlier pathos–bathos-drenched *Samsaram*. There were around a dozen characters—the father, mother, three sons, a daughter, a son-in-law, two daughters-in-law, and so on. There was a conscious attempt at distinct characterization of each one of them. I had access to the library at Gemini Studios which was also a kind of dumping ground for mountains of old files most of which were 'subjects' or stories proposed to be made into films in the future. One was a rather fully worked-out script bearing the byline of R.K. Narayan (ah!). Obviously, an R.K. Narayan had done a treatment for *The Three Sons* and it is very likely he didn't know what name the film would ultimately have. Like all its films, Gemini productions only had a serial number to identify them at the beginning. I think *The Three Sons* was production number 16 or 18 or 20 and got its filial name only about a fortnight before it was ready to be released. Even in 1952, the Narayan treatment was close to papyral disintegration; it must have been done a long many years before 1952 and more than half the number of sheets were missing in the file. But the opening scene was intact and it seemed quite interesting. Anyway, the film opened at a Madras cinema hall one summer afternoon and by the evening, it was declared a dud.

There was nothing seriously wrong with it but the audience just couldn't take another film about a family torn asunder in the fourth reel and reunited in the last. Of course, as was usual with the Gemini staff, we weren't prepared to believe that a Gemini film could actually fail after *Chandralekha*, *Nishan* and *Sansar*. But *The Three Sons* did. Then there was a film called *Parasakthi* starring a skinny, pop-eyed, loud-mouthed young man. His name was Ganesan. He would later be known as Sivaji Ganesan. He had played the role of Shivaji on the stage many years before his first film *Parasakthi* but the old achievements of a man are only glorified when he becomes a success. *Parasakthi* and Ganesan were a roaring success but Gemini had nothing to do with it! *Parasakthi* was a break from the hitherto-established Tamil film tradition. There were a great deal of contemporary elements in it; almost every line had an allusion to the political or social scene in Tamil Nadu. The makers of films like *Parasakthi* represented a real threat to the supremacy of Gemini Studios.

I played a respectably insignificant role in the huge Gemini machine of over 600 men and women. The women comprised of a dozen dance girls and a telephone operator. Some would call her an Anglo-Indian and some an Indian-Christian. She had one of the finest voices and remarkable English diction. She was a woman of immense patience and poise, and for some reason was (maybe, she's dead now) a spinster. In this movie kingdom of 600 subjects, my duty was to mutilate large numbers of newspapers and affix the clippings under a variety of heads from 'Aarey Milk Colony' to 'Zoroastrianism'. These were stored in cupboards of files. The mountains of magazines and trade journals to which Gemini Studios subscribed were not to be cut from, so I had to copy out in longhand thousands of news items, reports, articles and reviews from them. If Baburao Patel had only known how I rewrote the majority of his editorials and the 'Bombay Calling' pages of *Filmindia*, he would surely have made me an ingredient of his later-day homoeopathic preparation, *Shivsakthi* (which he qualified as 'the tonic of gods'). Anyway, next to the principal secretary of the prime minister, I was probably the most informed man in India and perhaps I was one better because I knew a couple of spies too.

Coming back to *The Three Sons*. When I watched the film fleeing from one cinema hall after another; I knew the Boss wasn't going to take it like the passive mother of the three sons in the film.

It is a curious thing how Vasan came to be called 'Boss' by everyone, including the members of his family. Smugglers hadn't got into Indian films (as characters), Amitabh Bachchan hadn't starred in *Don* and *Muqaddar ka Sikandar* and Vasan himself had never worn a trench coat, brandished a gun or chain-smoked cigars. But I understand he was called Boss almost from the time he came by Gemini Studios back in 1941. And I think I have a fairly acceptable explanation. Vasan's first deputy, the general manager of Gemini Studios, was an American by the name of William J. Moylan. I believe he and his wife lived on the Gemini lot and I have heard many stories, admiringly told, of the quality and quantity of attention the couple gave to the upkeep and maintenance of the studios. And it is very likely Moylan referred to Vasan as Boss, and since Moylan was so universally admired for his efficiency, imagination and sincerity, the nickname Boss caught on even after he left India and sailed home to put in his effort to America's war with the Axis.

Yes, Boss became even more determined to show everyone that Gemini was still the champ. So after doing a 'quickie' in Hindi, *Mr Sampat*, he plunged into completing a Tamil film that was virtually under production for eight years.

If you think a bunch of Aesop's fables would make a good whole film, then you are the man or woman to try and make *Avvaiyar*. There is a body of medieval Tamil poetry attributed to a female poet by the name of Avvaiyar but, as is usual with old heroes, poets, kings and queens, there is no definite and authentic record of her life and origin. There are a number of individual stories, unrelated to one another, with Avvaiyar as a character in them, but most of them are stories revolving around a single incident and unsuitable for a lengthy, sustained narrative. The veteran Tamil stage actor T.K. Shanmukam had done a successful stage play

of Avvaiyar but as a Tamil play it didn't pose
any special narrative problem because Tamil
drama then was made up of dozens of scenes
and each scene had a one-incident content.
So Avvaiyar on stage wasn't too unusual or
even commercially risky. I don't know who
sold the idea (or how Vasan bought the idea),
but Gemini announced *Avvaiyar* as one of its
forthcoming productions in 1944 or 1945. It
must have had a serial number less than ten,
but nobody seemed certain it would be made
into a viewable movie at any foreseeable time.
Vasan, however, declared around the close of
1952, shortly after his *Mr Sampat*, that *Avvaiyar*
would be the next Gemini release. He even
fixed the date: 15 August 1953.

*

My insignificant function in the Gemini
kingdom, although I was the most informed
person of the 600 subjects, didn't allow me to

participate directly in the making of *Avvaiyar*. But I had seen all that had been filmed of the lady until then. The birth of *Avvaiyar* ran for two hours. Her childhood took up another two hours. *Avvaiyar* renounces worldly life in the next two hours and meets a henpecked man over two hours. Her confrontation with a ghost lasted two hours. Sorry, four hours.

The lady is at the residence of a proverbially generous chieftain for another two hours. There were several such two-hour episodes. The fact is that whenever Vasan thought one among his 'ideas men' was oversleeping in the afternoons, he would tell him, 'Why not do a bit of *Avvaiyar*?'

Thousands of feet of film had been exposed, dozens of songs recorded, reams of dialogue written, spoken and recorded. Barring the central character of *Avvaiyar*, which was played by K.B. Sundarambal, the others were chosen from whoever was available from among the 600 in-house. And then Vasan sat down to

make a selection from the miles of footage—
only in films can the footage be in miles. He
sat through hours of projection of all that had
already been shot, and his editors stood by
with scissors and splicers. Every time he sat for
a while closing his eyes, it meant a thousand
feet were cut off. He streamlined multi-styled
rendering, freshly shot and inserted connecting
links from scene to scene, giving a truly poetic
beginning to the film, and ending the film with
a spectacular 'ascent to the heavens' finale.
Vasan worked like a man possessed and he
drove his 600-strong subjects to a state of
possession. Six months of feverish toil. Matters
which had remained undecided for six years
were decided in six seconds. Things that were
thought impossible were finished in a week.
In fact, the final version of *Avvaiyar* contained
more footage shot during the final six months
than any of the older footage shot over the
previous eight years. I was amazed that out of
a pile of sloppy stuff, such a streamlined and

interesting film could be made. Here was craft fine-tuned into an art.

*

From about the second week of July, Vasan set about planning the promotion of the film. Things had changed quite a lot since his last successful Tamil film. It was no longer enough if it was merely a Gemini film; no longer were mere full-page advertisements and giant hoardings going to assure big crowds. It was all right for mavericks to do films like *Parasakthi*; they could insult everybody and get away with it. Vasan and his like couldn't. The establishment was a jealous mistress.

Vasan had found a way to make the establishment a trump card in getting the most out of *Avvaiyar*. He couldn't have started his promotion campaign with a more emphatic symbol of the establishment than the chief minister of the state. The chief

minister of Tamil Nadu at that time was
C. Rajagopalachari, also known as Rajaji.
These days you can, with ease, get chief
ministers to act in films. But in 1953, for a
person like Rajaji to attend a preview of a
movie could be likened to Shrikant Verma
taking the salute at an RSS rally or Morarji
Desai presiding over a 'Made for Each Other'
smoking couples contest.

From around 1930, Rajaji and Vasan had
known and hated each other most cordially. At
that time, Vasan was still a 'rising' young man
in South India plunging into any field offering
speculation, and Rajaji was already a 'risen'
middle-aged politician who only gently lowered
himself into the water of the ordinary or
mundane when he could see the bottom level.
Vasan was 100 per cent a free-enterprise man,
taking things as they came, whether in races,
or book publishing and selling. He functioned
as an agent selling a thousand articles from
hair dye to 'automatic pistol—licence not

required'. He was also a magazine publisher, film distributor and finally a studio owner and film producer. Rajaji's past was an open book— so many books had been written about him— and whatever he said or did, one seemed to sense he was communicating only one thing— heads I win, tails you lose. His heart must have leapt with joy right out of his mouth when around 1930, a man like Kalki (pseudonym for R. Krishnamurthy), with enormous talent for articulation, a keen sense of humour, and a capacity for total devotion, hitched himself to Rajaji's cart. I cannot recall anybody in recent history anywhere in the world who possessed as astounding a versatility as Kalki. He proved a huge asset to Rajaji, the politician and the public personality from early in his career. When Vasan, after a couple of years, enticed Kalki to be the editor of his publication, *Ananda Vikatan*, Rajaji never forgave him for this act of 'stealing'. Although in the ultimate analysis, Rajaji was the one to have most benefitted, for after serving Vasan and his magazine for about ten years, Kalki returned to serve Rajaji all over again. The stint with Vasan had, meanwhile, given him an enormous stature.

In 1941, when Kalki broke from Vasan's magazine enterprise to start his own magazine, *Kalki*, Rajaji could not have asked for a more effective forum, or a more splendid spokesman. Kalki was now his own boss, after having established an incredibly wide and powerful rapport with the reading and thinking cross section of the Tamil populace through Vasan's *Ananda Vikatan*. For years after Kalki started his own magazine, Rajaji kept battering Vasan— his scathing criticism was ostensibly directed at him—for running a crossword puzzle competition, or for his political appraisals, or even his films (indecent, vulgar, unbelievable, childish, etc.). Vasan, through *Ananda Vikatan*, would retaliate by undermining Rajaji's part in the national political happenings, or by mocking any film M.S. Subbulakshmi acted in.

However, by 1953, both must have matured to admit the other's separate identity. Vasan scored a brilliant stroke by inviting Kalki to a private preview of *Avvaiyar*. I am sure Kalki must have been taken aback, but then he was taken in too. Long before the film was ready for any kind of public viewing, Kalki wrote a most elaborate and extravagant account of *Avvaiyar* in his magazine, titling the piece *'Kandariyathana Kanden'* (I've Seen Things Never Seen), meaning (very flatteringly, of course) that Vasan's *Avvaiyar* was something of a miracle. With one stroke, Vasan had made a bothersome rival his ally, and he had launched a novel film promotion campaign most auspiciously. Kalki's ecstatic response to *Avvaiyar* must have played upon the mind of his guru, Rajaji, so Vasan had no difficulty in getting the chief minister to his Gemini Studios' Preview Theatre 'A' a week before the scheduled release of the film. Rajaji, no mean employer of words, sat through the film in silence. After the film, his host and all his important colleagues watched with bated breath, as Rajaji walked to the car and left in silence. The fact was there for all the world to interpret: Rajaji had sat through *Avvaiyar*.

For the next one month or so, the Preview Theatre 'A' of Gemini Studios witnessed a galaxy of personalities watching *Avvaiyar* at special showings: important statesmen, politicians, educationists, members of the judiciary, legal luminaries, medical doctors, leaders of different language groups, prominent film producers, actors, musicians, writers, newspapermen, members of the legislative assembly and the council. It was doctors' day one day, engineers' day next, judges' day the third day, principals' day the fourth, and so on. Day after day, 5 p.m. onwards, I stood at the gate of the studios, wearing my oversized shirt and overstretched smile, welcoming the carloads of important men and women, and guiding them to the preview theatre. After the show, they were encouraged to say a few words and every word was registered in shorthand by someone and in longhand by me. The following day, the Madras newspapers would carry news of their reactions, columns about them, and before the film had run its first couple of weeks at the cinema halls, *Avvaiyar* was not just a movie but some kind of a cultural phenomenon. The ultimate in the great game of publicity and promotion came when a committee of prominent citizens of Madras got together under the chairmanship of Sir C.P. Ramaswamy Aiyer and publicly honoured Vasan for producing *Avvaiyar*. You should have heard Sir C.P. Ramaswamy Aiyer drowning Vasan under a deluge of panegyrics even though they sounded a little nineteenth-century. There were columns and columns of news reports about *Avvaiyar*.

Did I just say that this public felicitation was the ultimate in this *Avvaiyar* episode? No. On a quiet winter evening, the chief minister left his office, but not for home. The car stopped at the Wellington cinema hall on Mount Road. While the small, frail chief minister got out of the car and stood in the unimpressive foyer, the driver went in to buy a ticket. The show had just started. Just when Rajaji was about to climb the steps— the upper classes of seats in most cinema halls needed strong legs to take the stairs—someone noticed that this was no ordinary filmgoer. The manager came running out, the owner of the cinema hall soon joined the manager and the inevitable telephone call to Gemini Studios conveyed the unbelievable news that Rajaji was at Wellington to see *Avvaiyar* for a second time, this time paying for his ticket! A quarter of an hour later anyone who counted in the Gemini kingdom was at Wellington and I am sure Rajaji felt utterly distracted by all the fuss. I am sure he frowned behind his dark glasses.

Avvaiyar ran for a day less than six months at Wellington and it was succeeded by another Gemini film which proved a dud. The title of the film was *Rajee My Darling*. To the hero, maybe, but definitely not to the audience.

Incidentally, Rajaji's diary jotting for 10 August 1953 says a few more things. The complete text is as follows:

Saw Gemini Vasan's picture *Avvaiyar*. T.K. Shanmugam's play is a hundred times superior to this picture . . . A lot of stock scenes of thunder, lightning and storm, of water flowing and elephants trooping and cardboard fortresses falling. Avvai(yar) is too angry and cursing . . . The picture is poor but when so much has been spent on it and the stake is so great how can one frankly condemn it? The music is execrable! (10.8.53)

That was Rajaji.

Vasan died in 1968, a full fifteen years before the world would know what Rajaji truly felt about his film *Avvaiyar*. It was a bit of a surprise for me too—I had been foxed into believing that

Rajaji had liked the film. But I was relieved that Vasan had been spared the knowledge of the diary entry.

6

Never-never Land

Enticing Rajaji to see *Avvaiyar* twice wasn't the last thing Vasan did with that film. He used fairly large chunks of the film to compose a new Hindi film under the title *Bahut Din Huwe* which was to be the equivalent of 'Long, Long Ago'. For the first time, a Gemini film sported a real film star whom people in the north would readily recognize with a sigh or a gasp. The star was Madhubala.

I do not know whether Madhubala would pass for a breathtaking beauty among filmgoers today, but in the fifties, quite a few thought that she was the most beautiful girl India had ever seen in about forty years of movies and talkies in this country. Those who read *Filmindia*, which was about the only film magazine which commanded continued attention then, repeated the editor Baburao Patel's appellation for the girl: 'Venus of the Indian Screen'. If the real Venus really looked like *Venus de Milo* in the Louvre, then Baburao Patel wasn't far from right for among the top actresses of the day, and at her age, Madhubala was a little thick at the waist. Some said she was a very arrogant person, others said it was only her father.

She had managed to antagonize most of the film journalists who operated in Bombay then. The film she acted in as a child, *Basant*, ran for two years or so but after she attained her Venus title, no film of hers was a real hit. Someone might well ask, what about Kamal Amrohi's *Mahal*? If the film had run as much as the director of the film talked about it, it would have been a big success. Madhubala wasn't a very articulate person and I am sure even in the best of times, she aroused more pity than passion in people. After every kind of adventure and misadventure in a film actress's life, she died a sad, premature death.

When Vasan booked Madhubala for *Bahut Din Huwe,* she seemed to have already caught a bit of the forthcoming gloom. She was ill for most of the time the film was under production, and her parents, son, husband and abductor (in the film) all had to do their scenes with her but without her physical presence.

Her role in the film was also the quintessence of misery and misfortune. She is born a princess but loses her mother in a week. The stepmother keeps her busy all the time with mountains of brass vessels to be washed clean, and piles and piles of clothes to be washed white. Even for a royal household, the quantity of cooking vessels and clothes was a little too much. Her misery seemed to be at an end when a prince chances to see her and marry her. But a wicked lecherous magician kidnaps her and takes her away to his palace. The magician lives like a king, complete with fancy furniture and chandeliers, an army of servants of either sex and a full-fledged dungeon. Her husband and his men are turned into stone by the magician when they come to rescue her. She is thrown into the dungeon because she will not yield to the magician.

After several reels of every type of conceivable and inconceivable misfortune, she is reunited with her husband and son, but I do not know whether it came as a relief to the audiences. Who knew what would happen after this reunion? One could never be too sure with a princess played by Madhubala.

When Vasan decided to do the film and that too with Madhubala as the heroine, at least half of the Gemini kingdom of 600 came up with suggestions for whom to cast as the hero. No one suggested Dilip Kumar or Raj Kapoor but quite a few swore by Bharat Bhushan and a good number of people by Pradeep Kumar. I hope it is no comment on the ability of the two because for more than half the film, the hero stands as a statue made of stone. Ultimately, the two did come over to Gemini Studios to act years after their luminosity had begun to fade.

But Vasan in 1953–54 wasn't inclined to import outside talent. He got his own staff writer to do the dialogue and the lyrics; his staff musicians to compose music and play it; staff photographers, staff sound recordists, staff editors, staff publicity men, staff tailors, staff laboratory technicians, staff make-up men, staff gardeners, staff cooks, staff projectionists, staff ideas men and, above all, staff heroes, staff heroines and staff comic players of both sexes. So a staff actor became the prince in *Bahut Din Huwe*. His part in the film was all in brief flashes—meeting the princess, the wedding, the birth of a son, then the magician. From then on, he appeared as a stone statue.

As usual, the publicity department got down to work a couple of months before the date of the film's release. A special souvenir-like volume for the hundred-odd possible exhibitors of the film was readied. 'Long, Long Ago . . .' the text began. Extraordinary virtues were discovered and recorded in flamboyant language about each and every aspect of the film, with whole chapters about architecture, costumes, make-up and even lighting. I do not know whether any of the thousand cinema-hall managers or owners did anything more than look at the pictures in the volume. But the men in the Kohinoor building asserted in cold print without even seeing a frame of the film that Gemini had created yet another celluloid classic. The Kohinoor building housed the publicity and public relations department.

Bahut Din Huwe is one of Gemini's least-remembered films, or better still, most-forgotten film. But I remember it for two things. A gigantic Bengali gentleman—settled in Madras and for whom the Madras Race Club was a second home—kept hoping feverishly that he would be made the magician in the film. Like the racing tips he handed out to his friends and foes alike, this expectation also proved to be a horse which ran the other way. All he could manage was a tiny appearance, as one of the demons that waited on the magician. Literally painted black and blue and white all over, his lone scene in the film consisted of standing before Madhubala and trying frantically to frighten her. They said in Gemini Studios that that was the only day during her four months' stay in Madras when Madhubala smiled.

The other most memorable thing for me about *Bahut Din Huwe* is the group photograph of the Gemini 600 that was used as a centre spread for the souvenir. Imagine 600 clothed men and women as a centre spread! Vasan might have been able to construct his colossal extravaganzas with his own staff talent but this group photograph needed a puny outsider. One afternoon, the photographer had all the 600 lined up in about a dozen rows. Mentally splitting the group into two halves, he photographed the right. A colleague of mine thought they were two different photographs of the whole group and as he did not like his position in the first, after the first exposure was over, ran over to the other side and thrust his face in a gap.

When the two photographs were pasted together to contain the entire 600, it was one more than 600. Of course, no one noticed it; our heads were all like so many pinheads. Tennyson may not have been inspired but he might have wished for cannons to roar and thunder to the right and left and before and behind the 600.

Bahut Din Huwe, a magical film, vanished from the theatres like magic. Neither Madhubala nor the elephants of *Avvaiyar* could save the film. But there was still an old faithful—I think it was in Poona—and he ran the film for twenty-five weeks and won an endurance prize.

At that time, Vasan was trying to get *Chandralekha* and *Sansar* into the international circuits. I saw the international versions of both and have never felt more uneasy. India might have one of the lowest per capita incomes and an average Indian might statistically consume the fewest calories and enjoy the highest protein deficiency, but the leading ladies of both the films, at the time they participated in the films, were a visual antithesis of all that. They were a rage in India or else the two films couldn't have been all that successful.

But across the oceans, they activated a different kind of rage. Seeing *Chandra* (as the film was titled for the American audiences), a little boy had asked his utterly depressed father, 'Why don't the men use their guns?' Almost every male character in the film carries a gun, some as tall as six feet with permanently fixed bayonets, but whenever there is a fight, they fight with their fists or swords. One guard leans his gun against a wall so that he might fight better—with his fists. Not much news about the Japanese reaction to *Sansar*, retitled as *Such Is*

Life. I do not know whose idea it was to take the film to Japan. Maybe it was a delayed retaliation to the bomb Japan dropped on Madras during World War II.

But I have every reason to believe that the Boss wasn't really too keen on these international forays. No doubt he had a weakness for anyone who said he had spent some time abroad. Without any hesitation he would take him on his payroll and in his own sweet time think of some project to keep him occupied. I have a suspicion that the international versions of *Chandralekha* and *Sansar* were spoofs on more than one level. Vasan might even have planned it all as a joke on the Indian audiences.

In its particular category, *Bahut Din Huwe* was not a bad film. It had the unfailingly swift Gemini narration. The special effects cameraman Prahlad Dutt had, with the available equipment and resources (which were not much), worked out some extraordinary visuals. Hollywood had just then been thoroughly demoralized by the sweeping popularity of television, and was experimenting with widescreen and 3D film. It was to be a ghost story. He died so soon after making the announcement that some suspected he had gone to fix the location and cast for his film. *Bahut Din Huwe* had a very good background score and the veena-dominated orchestral piece composed by the then Gemini staffer Emani Shankara Sastry was exceptional. In the history of Indian films, there are many instances of songs being hits while the film flopped. But whoever heard or talked about *Bahut Din Huwe* or its music?

A few months after 'Long, Long Ago . . .' Vasan sent out another Hindi film disguised as made by somebody else. Titled *Do Dulhe*, it was a remake of a successful Tamil film. Perhaps this was a spoof too on both the Tamil audiences and the maker of the original Tamil film. *Do Dulhe* enjoyed the briefest of honeymoons. A number of cinema halls threw the film away even before the first week was over. It seems so callous to say so but that was the truth. The same crew and the same set of actors and actresses who had once in complete anonymity produced smashing successes like *Chandralekha*, *Nishan*, *Mangala* and *Sansar* were turning out one flop after another. If *Bahut Din Huwe* wasn't auspicious to the 600, *Do Dulhe* sounded the death knell.

In the summer of 1955, Vasan made a trip to Bombay. When he came back to announce the details of the next Gemini film, many couldn't believe their ears. It was obvious that from then on, it was stars, not the Gemini banner, that would be all important. Dilip Kumar, Dev Anand, Bina Rai, Vijayalaxmi, Jayant, Kumar. Vasan didn't stop with that. For dialogue, he signed on Ramanand Sagar who had been basking a little too long in the sunshine of Raj Kapoor's *Barsaat*; C. Ramachandra for music, Rajindar Kishan for lyrics. If it were not made in Madras, *Insaniyat*—that was the name of the next Gemini film—could well have been a film by Arora or Talwar of Mehboob or Filmistan.

I was rather raw and young and right in the thick of happenings to realize then that a significant phase in the history of Gemini Studios had come to an end. Vasan and Gemini continued to make films for many more years and even managed an occasional hit. But it was never like the old times—the days of 'Long, Long Ago . . .' and before.

7

Poets and Pancakes

Pancake was the brand name of the make-up material that Gemini Studios bought in truckloads. Greta Garbo must have used it, Miss Gohar must have used it, Vyjayanthimala must also have used it but Rati Agnihotri may not have even heard of it. The make-up department of Gemini Studios was on the top floor of a building that was believed to have been Edward Clive's stables. A dozen other buildings in the city are said to have been his residence. For his brief life and an even briefer stay in Madras, Robert Clive's son Edward seemed to have done a lot of moving, besides fighting some impossible battles in remote corners of India, and marrying a maiden at St. Mary's Church in Fort St. George in Madras.

The make-up room had the look of a hair-cutting salon with lights at all angles around half a dozen large mirrors. They were all incandescent lights, so you can imagine the fiery misery of those subjected to make-up. The make-up department was first headed by a Bengali man who became too big for a studio and left. He was succeeded by a Maharashtrian who was assisted by a Dharwar Kannadiga, an Andhrite, a Madras Indian Christian, an Anglo-Burmese and the usual local Tamils. All this shows that there was a great deal of national integration long before the AIR. and Doordarshan began broadcasting programmes on national integration. The gang of nationally integrated make-up men could turn any decent-looking person into a hideous crimson-hued monster with the help of truckloads of pancake and a number of other locally made potions and lotions. Those were the days of mainly indoor shooting, and only 5 per cent of the film was shot outdoors. I suppose the sets and studio lights needed the girls and boys to be made to look ugly in order to look presentable in the movie. A strict hierarchy was maintained in the make-up department. The chief make-up man made the chief actors and actresses look ugly, his senior assistant the 'second' hero and heroine, the junior assistant the main comedian, and so forth. The players who were part of the crowd scene were the responsibility of the office boy. (Even the make-up department of Gemini Studios had an office boy!) On the days when there was the shooting of a crowd, you could see him mixing his paint in a giant vessel and slapping it on the crowd players. The idea was to close every pore on the surface of the face in the process of applying make-up. He wasn't exactly a 'boy'; he was in his early forties, having entered the studios years ago in the hope of becoming a star actor or a top screenwriter, director or lyricist. He was a bit of a poet.

In those days I worked in a cubicle, two whole sides of which were French windows. (I didn't know at that time they were called French windows.) Seeing me sitting at my desk tearing up newspapers day in and day out, most people thought I was doing next to nothing. It is likely that the Boss thought likewise too. So anyone who felt I should be given some occupation would barge into my cubicle and deliver an extended lecture. The 'boy' in the make-up department had decided I should be enlightened on how a great literary talent was being allowed to go waste in a department fit only for barbers and perverts. Soon I was praying for crowd shooting all the time. Nothing short of it could save me from his lectures.

In all instances of frustration, you will always find the anger directed towards a single person openly or covertly, and this man of the make-up department was convinced that all his woes, ignominy and neglect were due to Kothamangalam Subbu. Subbu was the No.

2 at Gemini Studios. He couldn't have had a more encouraging opening in films than our grown-up make-up boy had. On the contrary, he must have had to face more uncertain and difficult times, for when he began his career, there were no firmly established film-producing companies or studios. Even in the matter of education, especially formal education, Subbu couldn't have had an appreciable lead over our boy. But by virtue of being born a Brahmin—a virtue, indeed!—he must have had exposure to more affluent situations and people. He had the ability to look cheerful at all times even after having had a hand in a flop film. He always had to work for somebody—he could never do things on his own—but his sense of loyalty made him identify himself with his principal completely and turn his entire creativity to his principal's advantage. He was tailor-made for films. Here was a man who could be inspired when commanded. 'The rat fights the tigress underwater and kills her but takes pity on the

cubs and tends them lovingly. I don't know how to do the scene,' the producer would say, and Subbu would come out with four ways for the rat to pour affection on its victim's offspring. 'Good, but I am not sure it is effective enough,' the producer would say, and in a minute Subbu would come out with fourteen more alternatives. Film-making must have been and was so easy with a man like Subbu around and if ever there was a man who gave direction and definition to Gemini Studios during its golden years, it was Subbu. Subbu had a separate identity as a poet and though he was certainly capable of more complex and higher forms, he deliberately chose to address his poetry to the masses. His success in films overshadowed and dwarfed his literary achievements—or so his critics felt. He composed several truly original 'story poems' in folk refrain and diction, and also wrote a sprawling novel, *Thillana Mohanambal*, with dozens of very deftly etched characters. He quite successfully recreated the mood and manner of the Devadasis of the early twentieth century. He was an amazing actor—he never aspired to the lead roles—but whatever subsidiary role he played in any of the films, he performed better than the supposed main players. He had a genuine love for anyone he came across and his house was a permanent residence for dozens of near and far relations and acquaintances. It seemed against Subbu's nature to be even conscious that he was feeding and supporting so many of them. Such a charitable and improvident man, and yet he had enemies! Was it because he seemed so close and intimate with the Boss? Or his readiness to say nice things about everything? In any case, there was this man in the make-up department who would wish the direst things for Subbu.

You saw Subbu always with the Boss but in the attendance rolls, he was grouped under a department called the Story Department comprising a lawyer and an assembly of writers and poets. The lawyer was also officially known as the legal adviser, but hardly anybody thought highly of his legal skills. An extremely talented actress, who was also extremely temperamental, once blew up on the sets. While everyone stood stunned, the lawyer quietly switched on the recording equipment. When the actress paused for breath, the lawyer said to her, 'One minute, please,' and played back the recording. There was nothing incriminating or unmentionably foul about the actress's tirade against the producer. But when she heard her voice through the sound equipment, she was struck dumb. A girl from the countryside, she hadn't gone through all the stages of worldly experience that generally precede a position of importance and sophistication that she had found herself catapulted into. She never quite recovered from the terror she felt that day. That was the end of a brief and brilliant acting career. The legal adviser, who was also a member of the Story Department, had unwittingly brought

about that sad end. While every other member
of the department wore a kind of uniform —
khadi dhoti with a slightly oversized and
clumsily tailored white khadi shirt—the legal
adviser wore pants and a tie and sometimes a
coat that looked like a coat of mail. Often he
looked alone and helpless—a man of cold logic
in a crowd of dreamers—a neutral man in an
assembly of Gandhiites and khadiites. Like so
many of those who were close to the Boss, he
was allowed to produce a film and though a lot
of raw stock and pancake were used on it, not
much came of the film. Then one day the Boss
closed down the Story Department and this
was perhaps the only instance in all of human
history where a lawyer lost his job because the
poets were asked to go home.

Gemini Studios was the favourite haunt of
poets like S.D.S. Yogiar, Sangu Subramanyam,
Krishna Sastry and Harindranath Chattopadhyaya.
It had an excellent mess which supplied good
coffee at all times of the day and for most part of

the night. Those were the days when Congress rule meant Prohibition and meeting over a cup of coffee was rather satisfying entertainment. Barring the office boys and a couple of clerks, everybody else at the studios radiated leisure, a prerequisite for poetry. Most of them wore khadi and worshipped Gandhiji but beyond that they had not the faintest appreciation for political thought of any kind. Naturally, they were all averse to the term 'communism'. A communist was a godless man: he had no filial or conjugal love; he had no compunction about killing his own parents or his children; he was always out to cause and spread unrest and violence among innocent and ignorant people. Such notions that prevailed everywhere else in South India at that time, naturally, floated about vaguely among the khadi-clad poets of Gemini Studios. Evidence of it was soon to come.

When Frank Buchman's Moral Re-Armament Army (MRA), some 200-strong, visited Madras sometime in 1952, they could not have found a warmer host in India than Gemini Studios. Someone called the group an international circus. They weren't very good on the trapeze and their acquaintance with animals was only at the dinner table, but they presented two plays in a most professional manner. Their *Jotham Valley* and *The Forgotten Factor* ran several shows in Madras; the Gemini family of 600 saw the plays over and over again. The message of the plays was usually plain and simple homilies, but the sets and costumes were first-rate. Madras and the Tamil drama community were terribly impressed and for some years almost all Tamil plays had a scene of sunrise and sunset in the manner of *Jotham Valley*, with a bare stage, a white background curtain and an accompanying tune. I am not sure however that this was indeed the case, for the unchangeable aspects of these big bosses and their enterprises remained the same, MRA or no MRA, international communism or no international communism. The staff of Gemini

Studios had a rare occasion hosting 200 people of all hues and sizes belonging to at least twenty nationalities. It was such a change from the usual collection of crowd players waiting to be slapped with thick layers of make-up by the office boy in the make-up department.

A few months later, the telephone lines of the big bosses of Madras buzzed and once again we at Gemini Studios cleared a whole shooting stage to welcome another visitor. All they said was that he was a poet from England. The only poets from England the simple Gemini staff knew or heard of were Wordsworth and Tennyson; the more literate ones knew of Keats, Shelley and Byron; and one or two might have faintly come to know of someone by the name Eliot. Who was the poet visiting Gemini Studios now?

'He is not a poet. He is an editor. That's why the Boss is giving him a big reception.' Vasan was also the editor of the popular Tamil weekly *Ananda Vikatan*.

He wasn't the editor of any of the known British publications in Madras, that is, those known at Gemini Studios. Since the top men of *The Hindu* were taking the initiative, the surmise was that the poet was the editor of a daily—but not from the *Manchester Guardian* or the *London Times*. That was all that even the most well informed among us knew.

At last, around four in the afternoon, the poet (or the editor) arrived. He was a tall man, very English, very serious and, of course, quite unfamiliar to all of us. Battling with half a dozen pedestal fans on the shooting stage, the Boss read out a long speech. It was obvious that he too knew precious little about the poet (or the editor). The speech was all in the most general terms but here and there it was peppered with words like 'freedom' and 'democracy'. Then the poet spoke. He couldn't have addressed a more dazed and silent audience. No one knew what he was talking about and his accent defeated any attempt to understand what he was saying. The

whole thing lasted about an hour; then the poet
left and we all dispersed in utter bafflement.
What were we doing? What was an English
poet doing at a film studio that made Tamil
films for the simplest sort of people? People
whose lives least afforded them the possibility
of cultivating a taste for English poetry? The
poet looked pretty baffled too, for he too must
have felt the sheer incongruity of his talk about
the thrills and travails of an English poet. His
visit remained an unexplained mystery.

The great prose writers of the world may not
admit it, but my conviction grows stronger day
after day that prose writing is not and cannot be
the true pursuit of a genius. It is for the patient,
persistent, persevering drudge with a heart so
shrunken that nothing can break it; rejection
slips don't mean a thing to him; he at once sets
out making a fresh copy of the long prose piece
and sends it on to another editor, enclosing
postage for the return of the manuscript. It was
for such people that *The Hindu* had published a

tiny announcement in an insignificant corner of an unimportant page: a short story contest organized by a British periodical by the name of *Encounter*. Of course, the *Encounter* wasn't a known commodity among the Gemini literati. I wanted to get an idea of the periodical before I spent a considerable sum in postage in sending a manuscript to England.

In those days, the British Council Library had an entrance with long-winded signboards and notices to make you feel like you were sneaking into a forbidden area. And there were copies of the *Encounter* lying about in various degrees of freshness, almost untouched by readers. When I read the editor's name, I heard a bell ringing in my shrunken heart. It was the poet who had visited Gemini Studios. I felt like I had found a long lost brother and I sang as I sealed the envelope and wrote out his address. I felt that he too would be singing the same song at the same time—long lost brothers of Indian films discover each other by singing the same song in the first reel and in the final reel of the film. Stephen Spender. Stephen Spender—that was his name.

And years later, when I was out of Gemini Studios and I had lots of time but not much money, anything at a reduced price attracted my attention. On the footpath in front of the Madras Mount Road Post Office, there was a pile of brand new books for fifty paise each. Actually, they were copies of the same book, an elegant paperback of American origin. 'Special low-priced pocket edition' in connection with the fiftieth anniversary of the Russian Revolution. I paid fifty paise and picked up a copy of the book, *The God That Failed*. Six eminent men of letters in six separate essays described 'their journeys into Communism and their disillusioned return': André Gide, Richard Wright, Ignazio Silone, Arthur Koestler, Louis Fischer and Stephen Spender. Stephen Spender! Suddenly the book assumed tremendous significance. Stephen Spender, the poet who had visited Gemini Studios! In a moment I felt a dark chamber of my mind lit up by a hazy illumination. The reaction to Stephen Spender at Gemini Studios was no longer a mystery. The Boss of Gemini Studios may not have much to do with Spender's poetry. But not at all with his god that failed.

8

Man, Music, Monkey

C. Ramachandra stood aghast. 'Sir,' he exclaimed, 'three bars of the opening orchestral music are gone!'

'Yes, yes. I know. I cut them,' said Vasan.

'Why, sir? And the first line of the song was sung three times. Now only one remains . . .'

'You mean the repetition of the pallavi. Why should there be three? Everybody will be able to follow the song.'

'It is not merely about following the song, sir. Each time it is sung differently. And again, there is no orchestral music between the second stanza and the third stanza.'

'Yes, Mr Ramachandra, I took that away. Doesn't it sound very good now?'

'But, sir, you have slashed the song into half.'

'No, Mr Ramachandra. I have only slashed it and made the scene effective. See it when the whole film is on screen, complete. You will find that the song has excellent tempo.'

There was no doubt about that. Vasan could make even a railway timetable have tempo. Only that with such tempo, you may not get the timings right all the time.

Ramachandra must have resigned himself to Vasan's methods. He liked Vasan, and Vasan liked Ramachandra, and their relationship went on sweetly–sourly for three major films beginning with *Insaniyat*, but I am sure every time Ramachandra gave a composition to Vasan, he felt like a man awaiting amputation.

It is not that Vasan didn't have the sensitivity to enjoy good music or dance. But for him a song or piece of music or a dance in a film must, more than anything else, be functional. This is probably the reason why, if one sat down to recollect all Gemini films, one realizes that no film (films like *Nandanar* and *Avvaiyar* included) stands out for music alone and no song lingers in the memory, outside the context of the film.

In 1955, C. Ramachandra, as a film music director, was at the very peak of his artistic and popular success. Taking off with *Khidki* and *Patanga*, along with *Samadhi*, *Sargam* and *Khazanalo Anarkali*, *Parchchain* and *Subah ka Tara*, Ramachandra had achieved excellence in variety and quantity. As films, most of these were inconsequential but Ramachandra's music stood out. Take the case of *Albela*. What would have ended as a second-grade Bhagwan–Baburao stunt film was transformed into a resounding film by the sheer melody of songs such as *Dheere se aaja* and *Balma bada naadan*. Not many know that Ramachandra, at the beginning of his career in the early forties, had composed the music for a Tamil film, again a kind of stunt film, titled *Vanamohini*. And a little before Vasan got him to do the music for *Insaniyat*, Ramachandra had had a smashing success with another South Indian film in Hindi, *Azad*. *Azad* must have been very much on his mind when Vasan went to Bombay to get a music director for his next Hindi film.

The year 1955, one realizes in retrospect, was a crucial one for Gemini Studios. Times were at last catching up with Vasan. If he wanted to be in business in a big way, as was expected of him, he would have to go the way of the rest of the 'big' moviemakers of India. Until then, in all his film projects, he was the man who made all the vital and not so vital decisions. Not bothering about anybody else's thoughts and views. All the commands and orders were his own, following his convenience and intuition; he was the supreme man as far as his film was concerned. He was the Boss. The scores of men and women needed for a film were all his employees who silently and devotedly did what they were asked to do at whatever month of the year, whatever time of the day.

But from the early fifties, he would have to take into consideration the whims and fancies of men and women who may not have had the slightest feeling for him, or may have been far less mature or wise, but who enjoyed at that moment the adoration of the film-going masses. In the process, Vasan had to jettison a number of gifted, devoted, and yet at that time, helpless people. For a good many of them, the end of their association with Gemini Studios also meant the end of their career. This was not the case only with writers, songwriters and music directors but also with actors, actresses and technicians. A Gemini man became so cut off from the rest of the world that for him, existence was almost impossible outside it. I am sure Vasan shed a few silent tears for them.

Pandit Indra, for instance. Vasan must have been so used to him, his black cap, zigzag walk, his unique sense of humour, his diabetes and his son-in-law. The Panditji for over five years and more than half a dozen films, wrote romantic scenes in the mornings, philosophical songs in the afternoons, proclamations of kings and commanders-in-chief in the evenings, and jokes and comic interludes at midnight. Give him a hint of an obscure Tamil proverb or saying, and he would provide the Hindi equivalent in a minute. At Gemini, all he had to do was translate or adapt from Tamil or Telugu originals and he himself had adapted to Gemini and Madras so well. He was an old-fashioned man—you could tell that by everything about him: his Calico Mills dhoti, his white full-sleeved shirt, the cap which folded like an oversized postcard and, of course, the slip-on shoes which must have been invented solely for Gujaratis. Apart from the translation and adaption work for the Hindi films of Gemini Studios, he did little. He wasn't particularly sociable, but when you keep seeing a quiet man every day over a period of years, you begin to like him and you begin to feel sympathy for him in his moments of difficulty. He was a small-dime western Indian Panditji all right, and he was being replaced by a pucca Bombay filmwalla, Ramanand Sagar, who wore immaculately tailored trousers, smoked expensive cigarettes and was, probably, a party swinger. The contrast, at least visually, was striking.

For a production with such stars as Dilip Kumar, Dev Anand and Bina Rai, music by C. Ramachandra and lyrics by Rajinder Kishen, *Insaniyat* was completed in a surprisingly short period of five months. Quite a number of players had to shuttle between Bombay and Madras at the shortest notice. After their bit of work for that schedule, they left Madras by an evening flight. Perhaps that was the only flight then. There had been occasions when someone came in by the morning flight, lunched in Madras and with the shooting cancelled, left for Bombay in the evening. Those were the happy days of carefree air travel—no airport admission fee, no security check, perhaps not even tickets. The pilots were so friendly with film actors and actresses that given a tip they seemed willing to delay the flight by a few minutes. The flight was at 5 p.m. but the shooting would go on and on. Someone from the studio would have gone to the hotel, packed the actor's luggage and brought it to the studio. At about 4.45 p.m. the car would zoom out of the studio with the actor still gloriously ugly in his make-up. On reaching the airport, both the actor and the driver would abandon the car and rush towards the aircraft. I had, on many occasions, feared that in the excitement the driver would be the one in the plane, leaving the actor on the runway, still trying to wipe off the paint on his face. Agha was a favourite with the crew and the airport staff, and so were Pran and Mehmood. I suppose all the actors and actresses were favourites—how else do you explain that not once had Gemini brought back someone because he or she had missed their flight? Crazy, crazy, we would all say and take satisfaction in misspelling the title of the film as 'Insanity'.

As had become customary with any Gemini production, *Insaniyat* was also the remake of another film. The original was a Telugu film with the title *Pallaturu Pilla*, meaning 'village girl'. It was a loose adaptation of Richard Sheridan's play, *Pizarro*. The Telugu film, in the tradition of Telugu films then, ran close to four hours, and *Insaniyat*, in order to be acceptable to the Hindi audiences, was planned to be about 15,000 feet—roughly three hours' duration. But an unforeseen development caused considerable change in the tightly worked-out script—all because of a monkey.

Fads and fancies are as much in evidence in films as perhaps in all walks of life. It was the beginning of a new trend of having performing animals in films. Usually, it was a dog or a horse or a cobra. Vasan had already used a dog in *Chandralekha*, not as a performing animal but to create an effect by its presence and a single bark.

Elephants competed with K.B. Sundarambal in *Avvaiyar*. When *Insaniyat* was about halfway through, Vasan said to his poet friends, 'If only there was an animal in the film.'

The poets remained silent but a generally reticent art director remarked, 'If a monkey ran about, people might like it.'

Everyone laughed. Not Vasan. Suddenly the whole room seemed to have heated up. The silence was now like one before a nuclear explosion. Vasan knitted his brow and asked, 'What did you say?

Thoroughly disoriented, the gentleman uttered, 'A monkey.' The meeting ended.

To anyone in India, the word 'monkey' would bring to mind images of troops of unruly monkeys around temples and sacred bathing ghats. Or a famished, helpless, outlandishly dressed creature the street juggler sometimes drags along, trained to salute and somersault for the passers-by. But to Vasan, it must have brought in thoughts of Tarzan and his

Cheetah. (Who could ever forgive Hollywood for naming a chimpanzee 'Cheetah'?) In spite of the Indian communication system, an overseas deal was struck and before the month was over, Zippy the chimpanzee and its trainer landed in Madras, straight from the US.

On first appearance, Zippy was an acute disappointment. No one knew how big a performing monkey ought to be, but everyone felt Zippy was too small, standing hardly a foot and a half from the ground. A fairly interesting part had been worked out for the creature but with such a midget, would it be credible? But then, one might ask, what indeed was credible in a film like *Insaniyat*?

But Zippy didn't do too badly. He posed for a number of publicity photographs, sporting a specially improvised pair of spectacles; reclining on a chair throwing his legs on the table and pretending to smoke a cigar big enough to send Samson reeling. Zippy stayed in Madras for about a month, arriving when the making of the film was halfway through and leaving when the end was still some way to go. So Zippy's participation, though adequate in the climax scenes, was lopsided, for he was totally absent in a number of other scenes. Many distinguished citizens of Madras and their families wanted to see Zippy in flesh, fur and blood, and we obliged them as much as we could. Scenes featuring Zippy were done with the camera placed slightly lower than eye level. Not many could tell that the animal was a little too small for all the exploits it was shown to have performed. *Insaniyat* would have been a powerful as well as an entertaining film even without Zippy. In fact, Zippy only succeeded in reducing quite a few dramatic scenes into farcical ones.

For some reason, in spite of Zippy and Agha, the film had a heavy, brooding quality. Even the acting of the supporting players was hammed. Kumar is depicted in the court of wicked Jayant, as a captive with a dozen spears thrust into him in a semicircle. He is asked the simplest of questions requiring the briefest of answers but he starts off with a long, pompous peroration on the nature of the earth, the composition of the stars, the topography of the heavens, and, of course, the damnedest thing, the human soul. It is difficult to tell between Jayant and Kumar who the captive is, and who the torturer. The one person whose acting was realistic was Dev Anand, but unfortunately he was made to sport a moustache that made him look more silly than heroic. He also had to do the very unpopular act of stealing Dilip Kumar's girl. The audiences kept booing Dev Anand all the time. But the advantage of being a film actor is that you don't have to take the rotten eggs in person.

Insaniyat was originally scheduled to be released on the first of October but was advanced by a day. As was customary with Gemini films, Calcutta was among the first places to screen the film. Bina, Basusree and one other cinema hall ran the film. Perhaps Hind or Jaihind. The editing department and laboratory and, of course, the projection theatre worked round the clock for weeks. Vasan still had these devoted men to stand by him and work sleeplessly for the hundred big and little things that complete a film but such people are rarely noticed outside the film community. Vasan with a retinue of close associates went to Calcutta to attend the premiere.

August and September 1955 were busy months for Hindi cinema lovers. Within intervals of a week and fortnight, three big Hindi films descended on them, and pretty soon it was evident that a kind of race between these three giants was inevitable. The three films were Shantaram's *Jhanak Jhanak Payal Baaje*, Raj Kapoor's *Shree 420*, and the third was *Insaniyat*. *Jhanak Jhanak* had had a couple of weeks' lead over the other two and was already being looked upon as a cultural grace brought to earth by the messiah, Shantaram. *Shree 420* was slick and sophisticated and was probably the only one among the three to have some kind of character development, building up of situations, and so on. *Insaniyat* depended on the audience's spontaneous recognition of the hero, heroine or villain, and viewers rushed forth to follow their good fortunes and misfortunes. In spite of the sombre tone of the film and a surfeit of hamming from almost all actors, when it was released on the thirtieth of September, it was expected to sweep past the other two rivals by sheer star power and the breakneck speed of the Gemini narration—the tempo Vasan was trying to educate Ramachandra about. A good number of people placed heavy bets on Zippy. But it was *Jhanak Jhanak* which settled down to a long run in cities across the length and breadth of the country. Quite some distance behind trudged *Shree 420* and *Insaniyat*.

But all this was among peers, men of the same flock. Vasan, Shantaram and Raj Kapoor were all products of the same system, members of the same milieu. Such men usually avoid collisions with one another and take care that they space their onslaughts on the filmgoers, but it was a rare coincidence in 1955 when they happened to storm the country with their blockbusters at the same time. Something else was happening at the same time.

The release of *Insaniyat* at Calcutta theatres was contracted long ago and in the interim period, before its release, the theatre was screening an odd film which people didn't know much about but were certain wouldn't run long. Besides being made by a newcomer who had nothing to do with the established film industry, the film had none of the usual ingredients which go into making a film in India. But as the deadline for the release of *Insaniyat* was nearing, the other film was proving to be an embarrassment—it was so good and was running very well. Vasan knew nothing about the film or its maker and just insisted on the contractual obligations. So, on the thirtieth of September, the film was withdrawn to make way for the Gemini film. But when Vasan saw the other film and came to know about its maker, he must have felt genuinely sorry. On returning to Madras, it was the other film he kept talking about. It was not his cup of tea—he wouldn't consider it tea at all—but he esteemed it highly.

It was a holiday. I think it was Deepavali. A place of work, particularly when it is a huge sprawling one like a factory or a film studio, exudes a strange, haunting charm on the days it doesn't work. I hadn't developed any particular liking for strange and haunting charms, but I went to the studio that day in the afternoon to do a bit of prosaic typing. I found the projection theatre open and impulsively entered it and sat on a vacant chair to realize a second later that Vasan and his close associates were watching a film. Presumably, it was half-time. The door closed and the film recommenced. The film was something I had known nothing about; I didn't know the language but I found myself throbbing with a surge of emotion, such as

I had never experienced before. The film was over but Vasan ordered it to be run again. I felt ever so grateful. Here was a chance to see the film in its entirety. I am sure I wasn't the only one in the theatre to be so deeply, so completely moved. Vasan's face revealed nothing but there he was, seeing the film all over again. When the film was finally over, I had to be alone and so I walked all the way back home.

That was the film that crossed *Insaniyat*'s path in Calcutta. It was called *Pather Panchali*.

9

Synthetic Smile

Normalcy at Gemini Studios wasn't possible after Vasan brought the sky down in 1955 with his star-filled *Insaniyat*. Consequently, one would have anticipated the establishment to continue in the same breakneck speed. But exhaustion set in.

The long-threatened reorganization and retrenchment took place. At any given time in the past, there was always someone who was regarded as the alter ego of the Boss, the apple of his eye. But now, nobody felt that way. It was not just a sense of security, but a pragmatic understanding that in that world of make-believe, no one was indispensable. The studio was beginning to change even physically. A part of the century-old colonial building was being pulled down mainly to provide the structure with a roof at a more manageable height and facilitate effective air-conditioning. A huge shed was razed to the ground to make way for a new box-like building to house the laboratories and the editing department. They hastily constructed a part of it so that Vasan could temporarily shift his office from the stately room in the colonial building—they said he sat in the very place Clive sat; and for months he found himself in a claustrophobic room eventually intended for 'outside' editors. Thinking of it now after thirty years, the event seems rather parabolic.

The floors remained empty and idle, the technicians who had prepped for retrenchment were discovering the delights of horse races at Guindy (Guindy is to Chennai what Mahalaxmi is to Mumbai) and afternoon naps, and the studio vehicles were being sent for lengthy, long-overdue repairs, but there was no sign of a new production in any language, Tamil or Hindi. The one department that seemed as busy as ever was accounts. In fact, they took in an additional hand and we all hoped they would do more additions than subtractions. I went about in a mad, merry way, collecting titbits of information, statistics, and reviews of all films—good, bad and indifferent—attending weddings, betrothals and funerals. I also turned away wave after wave of visitors from the gates of the studio with a terminology William Burroughs would have been proud to have created on one of his trips.

The matter of visitors to the studio must have been bothersome for Vasan. It was not only the reputation of the Gemini banner that drew unceasing crowds to its gates. It was so accessible—right in the heart of the city on one of its main arteries; visitors to the city as well as residents passed through it unfailingly every day. When for a while an American was Vasan's general manager, he had placed a signboard at the entrance to the studio that read—'This is not a picnic or sightseeing spot. Serious work goes on here.' Once the American was gone, one of the first things Vasan did was shove this signboard under a pile of castoffs, mostly files. And when he got a well-read, information-hungry, tight-lipped young man to work for him, he made him organize a public relations department that took care of the assault of the visitors. Most people thought the department did only this, which was no contribution to any of the resoundingly successful films the studios made. So we of the public relations department were always the low-key people, took a back seat in all the group photographs if we appeared at all, and chose shoes that didn't squeak. But we were the people who sent out the most letters from the studio. Barring the business letters, the whole bag of the studio's mail was turned over to us and we threw no letter out; no query or request, however impossible or childish, was left unanswered. The answer in effect was 'no' in almost all cases, but the form we gave it in was a masterpiece of abstract obfuscation. 'While being deeply grateful to you for the keen interest evinced by you, we are extremely sorry that the nature of our work does not permit requests like the one in your letter to be met in a mutually convenient manner. We trust you will appreciate our position . . .' This silenced several hundred thousand letter-writers and callers at the gate and on the telephone. When uttered without batting an eyelid, the message produced sepulchral silence and a profound bewilderment in the most ardent of fans who had so eagerly come to look at the place which had stirred their imagination with a string of film fantasies. We used a couple of variations of the statement but 'the nature of work' and 'mutually convenient manner' remained constant salvos against which the people of the land found themselves completely helpless. Someone could have asked what was so special about the nature of our work or could have said he didn't mind any inconvenience, but it never happened.

But a film studio can't afford to turn everybody out. It can't take chances with guests of income-tax commissioners and cousins of joint secretaries. Also of traffic constables. Or the airlines people. With no production and nothing really to show them, I told them the most fantastic stories about the empty sound stages and let them sit on the swivel chairs of the make-up rooms and told them, 'This is the very mirror Madhubala sat in front of.' Visitors could never resist the temptation to adjust their hair.

A small but significant number of really influential people succeeded in taking a look at the studio. They were far from the usual film-addicted, star-struck lot. In fact, some of them might not have seen a film in years but would have heard of Gemini in other contexts and become curious to know how exactly the infamous thing called a motion picture was being created. Such visitors were most disappointed to learn that scrap wood and wastepaper were the basic materials for all the dream worlds shown in a cinema. But a public relations man wasn't expected to send any visitor back disappointed or disillusioned. I told them fancy stories, things I had seen and heard, also things I had not seen but only heard. Vasan hadn't been only a film-maker. He had been a salesman, publicist, writer, publisher, owner of racehorses, and a strong nationalist, as his weekly publication affirmed. He donated such a large sum for the Kasturba Fund that Dr Rajendra Prasad came down to Madras to receive it in person. Vasan wore khadi, celebrated his daughter's wedding on a scale unseen and unimagined in Tamil Nadu, delighted in arranging big feasts, and had restored a dilapidated temple in his home village. He was a proverbially devoted son to his mother. From his long list, even the most unresponsive of guests could be made to stumble on some trait that touched him and my task was to trace it and revolve my talk around it.

Two men once turned up at the gates and just could not be turned away with the 'nature of work' rigmarole. There was something special about them and it was possible to sense that they had a secret mission in seeing a film studio. They lingered at the oddest places, the garden, for instance. After a leisurely hour, they must have felt it safe to tell me that they had come from Delhi to investigate the theft of a pair of rare lovebirds presented to the prime minister.

'You have birds, do you?'

'Yes, a few peacocks . . .'

'No, smaller ones. Birds which can fly . . .'

'We have a few birds which walk though we call them nightingales. We have so many of them in the South, I wish some of them would learn to fly and go into space.'

Most visitors found piles of dismantled sets and used costumes sufficiently exciting but the real VIPs couldn't be bluffed that way even if they did not have the inclination or time to witness actual film shooting. Unlike the other studios of Madras, Gemini was more or less exclusively for Vasan's productions. A producer of Telugu films and a model of monumental patience was the only other customer who used the studio and it is a wonder he managed to get his quota of one film a year completed in spite of the bulldozing priority always given to Gemini productions. There were many days on which no shooting took place, but it caused no concern or anxiety because one knew that a week or a month hence this seeming inactivity would be more than compensated by frenzied work.

There was this new group which had just made a film and was halfway through the second one. They were to do all their work at some other studio in Kodambakkam, but there was a piece of urgent work that really couldn't be rushed. It was one of the selling points of the

119

Ashokamitran

film—a big song–dance number with a horde of girls. Would it be possible to accommodate them just for this dance?

That came in handy as suddenly the Chinese premier, Zhou EnLai, felt his visit to India wasn't complete until he had had a peep into the Gemini Studios. The austere leader of the world's highest socialist state sat through an hour's shooting of a dance by a large princess wriggling with abandon in the company of her numerous companions—all as part of a revolution in an imaginary state to dispossess a bad king and install another in his place. It was all rather loud—aurally and visually—with the girls displaying jewellery on all possible parts of their bodies. The premier didn't seem to be particularly impressed with the story though he gave a faint smile when requested to stand for a photograph with the dancer.

Barely a fortnight after Zhou's visit, we once again got busy, preparing to receive another VIP group. This time it was the Lamas—the

Dalai and the Panchen. It was a time when Tibet hadn't yet become an issue but it was apparent while the spiritual head and the temporal head demanded to visit as a team, it wasn't exactly so. We were given an elaborate set of instructions about our conduct during their visit: the two would arrive separately and there would be two separate welcome functions with just half-hour interval between them. There must be garlands but no garlanding. You could only hand the garland over to the dignitary. Try as we did, it was impossible to keep the two groups completely isolated. As a matter of fact, where so many others failed, Gemini succeeded in bringing the two together. Again the same dancer and her dancing mates. If the Chinese premier's entourage could fill a large-sized bus, the Lamas seemed adequate for a train, and seating them all in the shooting took all the chairs in the studios. No one attempted to give a synopsis of the story. Perhaps some could have shouted out loud enough to reach the hundred-odd gathering, but the interpreter was too soft-spoken.

Days, weeks, months and it was soon to be a whole year since *Insaniyat* and there was still no sign of the next Gemini production. We were worried. And we stayed worried for a long time.

10

When Dust Choked
the Gemini Bugles

Insaniyat was like a space rocket burning up. In a short time, a mountain of money conserved over a long period had been burnt up. All that was left after take-off were a few seconds of a vaporous trail in the sky caused by the self-immolating rocket. We watched the trail for a long time even after it had vanished. Or, was there a trail at all?

Some old men at Gemini Studios had to go home and some had to accept a cut in their salaries. Some not-so-old men became new heads of departments. That apart, so little was happening and few knew what was happening.

With Shantaram's *Jhanak Jhanak Payal Baaje* thundering over the distant corners of India, everyone said there was no future for Gemini Studios if we didn't go in for colour. Barring a few films which had prints by Technicolor in London, the thing available in India then was a process called Gevacolor which made the whole process of film-making a kind of watery activity. The colour looked so washed up. It was all right in those days to have just a couple of reels in this Gevacolor and these two reels were packed with every conceivable dance and music. It was Hemantha Kumar in one film, C. Ramachandra in another, S.N. Tripathi in the third. Chubby-cheeked Mahipal in balloony pants swished and twirled his sword as a Gevacolor Alibaba, and Shakila was his wily and willing Morjiana (wonder why they named her so?). A South Indian film producer straightaway announced that he was making a Gevacolor Alibaba film himself, the first all-colour film in Tamil. Who was to play Alibaba? M.G.R., of course.

But nothing happened at Gemini Studios. There was a brief flutter when the head of 20th Century Fox (or Fox), Spyros P. Skouras, visited India and met Vasan at Gemini Studios. A co-production with Fox, colour and cinemascope, said the papers. In fact, Gemini circulated the news but those who knew what was happening, knew it wasn't serious. Vasan was content with victories over the Indian audiences. And he had a neat five hundred million of them to be won over.

It was this long period of lull after *Insaniyat* that should have permitted Vasan the luxury of being the fond husband and the fond father that he was. His devotion to his mother was proverbial to all those who knew him and she was so full of wisdom and goodness. There were many people who thought Vasan became a little tight-fisted only after the passing away of his mother. He was her only son. Life had been very cruel to her and the worst that could befall a poor Brahmin girl had happened to her—she became a widow when not yet twenty, with a child barely a few months old. Her courage, determination and rectitude were typical of an Indian woman of those years. Working herself to the bone, she brought up her son, gave him an education which she herself could never possess and intuitively guided him to a growing prosperity which was always accompanied by large-heartedness.

Vasan celebrated the wedding of his daughter in 1950 when the whole of India was spellbound by his string of smash hits, *Chandralekha*, *Nishan* and *Mangala*. It was still the time of rationing of all kinds, and things were really scarce. But the world would not have the maker of *Chandralekha* trading excuses.

For years, they spoke of Vasan's daughter's wedding as the grandest event the city of Madras had ever witnessed. For a whole week in 1950, the citizens of South Madras saw the moon at noon, the sun at midnight, men walked sideways on a hand and leg, birds stood as lamp posts, the choicest music crystallized into diamonds, the smell of the most extravagant South Indian vegetarian food hung heavily in the air that people breathed, the cows and buffaloes of Madras forgot to graze, the *jutka* (or carriage) horses danced the polka, and the waves of the Bay of Bengal stood still at their highest point to watch the fun. I wasn't there at the wedding but I knew every bit of it because the wedding was filmed in its entirety by the army of Gemini technicians, and I saw the miles of footage a few hundred times in the discharge of my professional duties. For months, the editors of Gemini Studios worked on the project called 'The Marriage Reel' and finally ended up with two versions—a two-reel wedding and a more leisurely and detailed four-reel wedding. Guests of Vasan, if they happened to be his relations and close friends, viewed the marriage reels as part of their visit to Gemini Studios. Since it was an event a few years old, it was an interesting thing to identify the numerous friends and employees of Vasan from what they looked like at the time of his daughter's wedding. One short, spectacled gentleman could be seen in almost all the frames of the marriage reels—his screen time far exceeded that of even the bride and bridegroom. There he was, shoving the crowd to make way for Vasan, waving the edge of his towel to provide a breeze for the Boss, or just looking at the big man with admiration. A man who seemed such a willing personal attendant to Vasan but was the first one to get the axe in the retrenchment, and they said some discrediting things about him too. So when I kept showing the reels to new guests, I couldn't help ruminating each time on that gentleman, on the impermanence of not only men and things but reputation and qualities. The wedding was an elaborate four-day festival—the choicest musicians, the choicest dancers and the choicest nagaswaram players provided the best of South Indian art to a multitude who were fed in batches of forty-nine to respect the rationing rules which forbade a feast for fifty or more persons. Vasan had bought a new mansion especially for the wedding. He named it Gemini House. There and on the giant floors of his studios and the prayer halls of a few nearby schools, the feeding went on non-stop. A traditional South Indian wedding has a few functions where the women of the bride's family and those of the groom's exchange pleasant musical banter and gently tease one another. The Gemini's *asthana* poet, Kothamangalam Subbu, wrote some of the finest songs for the occasion. These and the nagaswaram of the nagaswaram genius T.N. Rajarathnam Pillai and the vocal performance by the inimitable singer, the late G.N. Balasubrahmanian, filled one half of the marriage reels in both the long and short versions. The final cutting of the marriage reels was done by R.K. Ramachandran, none other than the brother of R.K. Narayan and R.K. Laxman.

In 1956, during the long lull after the release of *Insaniyat*, Vasan celebrated another wedding, this time of his son Balasubramanian, also known as Balu. The bride was a girl of Balu's choice and unlike Balu who had only one sister, the bride had several sisters and a brother. (It is a coincidence that Vasan's son-in-law too was born with a number of sisters and a brother.) We were told there were one or two older sisters to Balu's bride-to-be who were still to be married, and in a traditional South Indian Brahmin family, the marriage of a younger daughter would mean virtual spinsterhood for the older daughters if they were still unmarried. So the elder sisters of Vasan's daughter-in-law-to-be were also married off the same month, a few days before Balu's wedding. A huge pandal was erected at the large vacant site where the Music Academy Hall now stands, and all the staff of Gemini Studios as well as those of Vasan's other concerns joined together to see that no detail of the wedding was left to any ad hoc arrangement. Vasan had felt that during his daughter's wedding, many of his own intimate friends and compatriots hadn't received appropriate attention. So for nearly a month after the wedding, he had them over to his house for dinner, night after night.

There couldn't be a Gemini wedding without new clothes for the staff, and the leading silk sari manufacturers of the South had an excellent opportunity to clear their stocks, old, new and indifferent. I got only a dhoti and *angavasthram*, but the married staff got a silk sari as well. It was just about the time plastic was getting to be fashionable and the new clothes were distributed to the staff in a specially made rosewood box with a sliding plastic top on which was written: 'With the Best Compliments of Mr and Mrs Vasan on the occasion of the wedding of their son Balasubramanian with Saroja on 5th June 1956'. A silk sari is a very personal possession, and even the most docile Tamil girl will have her own ideas of the ideal sari for her. The rosewood boxes distributed in hundreds among the staff naturally contained saris that some recipients didn't like, and when someone mentioned this to Mrs Vasan, she said, in innocence, that people could exchange what they were given from a pile of saris at Vasan's residence that had not yet been distributed. They say that never in the history of Madras were so many women, each clutching a sari, seen huddled under one roof, spacious though Gemini House was. All wedding preparations came to a standstill following this siege by sari-selecting women. The next day a circular was sent around: 'No sari exchange.'

In 1956, the nagaswaram maestro T.N. Rajarathnam Pillai was very ill. So Vasan had asked Karukurchi Arunachalam to perform at the wedding. Arunachalam was a great artiste in his own right but on the wedding day, early in the morning, a car wriggled through a number of obstacles to stop at the main entrance of the marriage pandal and out stepped Rajarathnam Pillai, resplendently dressed! The great musician slowly made his way to the platform set apart for the nagaswaram players. He said, 'Ayyarveettumuhurthathukku naan vaasikkamayaaroodarathu?' (For a wedding in Iyer's house—meaning, Vasan's son's marriage—who but me would play the nagaswaram?) Vasan hurried to greet Rajarathnam, who had by then picked up his instrument to play. Not long afterwards, Rajarathnam died, his unsurpassable music enshrined in a few recordings. He must have been terribly ill even as he walked up to the platform at Vasan's son's wedding, but he had scrupulously put on the traditional silk attire and jewellery for the occasion.

His son's wedding must have brought memories of the daughter's wedding over and over again to Vasan. Only six years separating the two big moments of his family but how much the world had changed. Even he, the great Vasan, couldn't manage to get a great show going any longer. The son's marriage, though spectacular, wasn't a patch on the other one.

Vasan must have found himself dwelling more and more on the earlier times. Ah, *Chandralekha*! Ah, *Nishan*! Ah, *Mangala*! Dazzling women, gorgeous palaces, galloping horses, the swish of rapiers criss-crossing against a taut musical score. Vasan had made up his mind about the next film.

The announcement came shortly afterwards; he was reviving an old project. Vyjayanthimala, Padmini, Gemini Ganesan, Pran and Meenaxi would feature in it. C. Ramachandra would compose the music. Once again forts and moats, palaces and ships, horses and women would dazzle on film. A spectacle to celebrate all spectacles. *Raj Tilak*. In Tamil, *Vanjikottai Valiban*.

It was the last time Vasan yielded to his obsession to make a second *Chandralekha*. Of course, he couldn't, for everyone now knows that *Raj Tilak* was the biggest flop Gemini ever made. The cycle had indeed come to an end.

11

The Householder
Is Not a Simple Person

I do not think the technicians of Gemini Studios were ever briefed about an outsider as much as in the case of Kishore Sahu. *Dil Apna aur Preet Parai*, the film Sahu directed for Kamal Amrohi, was running very well at that time. We at Gemini Studios had gotten used to seeing strange faces on the sets without an inkling of what the possessor of the face was supposed to do for the film under production. So we felt rather strange when the Boss told the technicians in advance: 'Look here, I am getting a new director for this film. He is a terrible

135

sucker for punctuality. I do not want him to complain to me about any of you.'

Actually if the Boss had to be concerned about anything, punctuality should not have featured on his list. Shooting meant pick-ups and drops for all staff except those falling under the Factories Act. Then, food came from New Woodlands which, even today, is one of the best restaurants in Chennai. So the warning was really for those responsible for the transport management. I was the unacknowledged transport manager.

Sahu must have been quite perplexed at the excessive officiousness of the whole crew. Nature had given him a puzzled countenance and Gemini Studios made him look even more puzzled. Probably to ensure his own punctuality, Kohinoor was readied for his residence.

Kohinoor is a two-storeyed building connected to the main studio by a narrow pathway. It was bought from a neighbour who must have designed the place as a very private space and so allowed very little ventilation to any part of the structure. There were a number of small rooms, and for Sahu, each was furnished and fitted with an oversized ceiling fan. The result was that when Sahu and his family had all the fans switched on, the Kohinoor gave out a drone so large in magnitude that it turned conversation into a kind of shouting match.

Sahu might have been unknown to most Gemini staff but I had seen two of his films, *Kalighata* and *Mayurpankh*. Both seemed a bit narcissistic. Baburao Patel of *Filmindia* always ridiculed him, and Dev Anand indirectly fed fodder to that critic by making Sahu act in his film. So when Sahu sent word to me, I was worried about my inability to forget what Patel had said of Sahu and even if I did that, I could not forget Sahu in *The Guide*. In my initial meeting with him, I really had a difficult time trying to stifle my paroxysms.

The fact is that Sahu had aspirations beyond the celluloid realm. He had studied literature for his degree and had written fiction. When I met him in 1963, he had three published books in Hindi. He wanted his stories to be rendered into English and Tamil. When he mentioned this to our own Gemini Panditji, Melattur Vishwanathan, I became the candidate for the English translation. Sahu's target in English was to get at least one story published in the *Illustrated Weekly of India*, which until 1970 was the closest a writer could be to winning the Nobel Prize. I had won my 'Nobel' in 1961.

In 1963, when Sahu came to Madras to direct Gemini's *Grihasti*, he was nearing fifty. His wife and daughters were a picture of refinement, and Sahu never raised his voice. I believe he had a broken first marriage and maybe that had an effect on his voice. I had difficulty following him not because of his voice but because of the numerous long pauses he made whenever he spoke.

My reading ability of Hindi was very limited and matched Sahu's articulation. So

Vishwanathan and I sat together, and I managed to translate five of Sahu's stories into English. They were quite good, but nothing came out of them. If the successors of Sahu rummage in his old papers, they are sure to find *Grazia*, *Siraj Sahranpur* and *On the Telephone* in my handwriting. Sahu had said he would get them typed in Bombay and would personally take them to the editor of the *Illustrated Weekly*.

Grihasti progressed slowly and steadily. It had far too many characters needing to speak, and Boss had to get actors from Bombay by the dozen. The children were the most difficult part. And it turned out the censors did not like the children discussing their parents as in a mock parliament.

As the film progressed, the punctuality factor became a casualty and so was Sahu's hold on the film. Very likely, Vasan played a joke on us about Sahu being a stickler for punctuality. Invariably, the shooting ended around two in the morning and so Sahu would be the only one awake at 7 a.m., the official hour of the start of the next day's call-sheet.

Despite being deposited in the Kohinoor building close to six months and enduring 'home-cooking' by a cousin of one of Gemini's drivers, Sahu continued his association with Vasan. He had been long enough in the film industry to know that producers were compulsive back-seat drivers. He didn't get to direct another Gemini film but scripted two for which I wrote the dialogue.

I left Gemini Studios soon after. I am not sure if I was paid for my translation work. Sahu would have certainly compensated me for my efforts if only the editor of the *Illustrated Weekly of India* had published at least one piece of his. Nobel prizes are hard to come by.

12

I Attend a Premiere

There is a pattern in their deaths—Nadira, Suraiya, Devika Rani. They had all died alone with no kith and kin around them. There was a person to take care of their personal needs but how well, we do not know.

These celebrities didn't die in want. But there is something painful about their last days. Devika Rani lay limp in her bed, unable to speak. Her vast out-of-town Thataguni Estate bungalow with all its antique furniture and countless objects of art was considered inappropriate to see her through and she was shifted to a Bangalore hotel. The lady upon whom Devika Rani had become completely dependent produced a will and said she was the sole heir to all of Devika Rani's possessions. A life marked by a passion for living, for pioneering of a new art form, for nurturing histrionic talents of dozens of people and, above all, the gift of an extraordinary persona—all vanished within the four walls of a synthetically elegant city hotel.

I saw Devika Rani twice in her lifetime—once in 1964 and the second time in 1980. Maybe the second meeting needs to be narrated first.

It was at the 'Filmotsov' in Bangalore. A person who was thought to be politically pulverized in 1977 materialized, vanquishing all her antagonists humiliatingly. All the Lok Sabha elections results hadn't been declared but it was clear which way they were gravitating. The film festival with the fancy name of 'Filmotsov' that year seemed entirely of the officials, for the officials, by the officials. Not a single minister from Delhi or Karnataka found the occasion worthy of gracing with his or her presence.

The officials found the nearby celebrity, Devika Rani, amenable. The traditional lighting of the lamp had not been invented yet and it was enough if the special guest spoke a few words.

Devika Rani arrived at the appropriate time. Suddenly there was a strange kind of commotion and shouting of slogans as she was escorted inside the cinema hall. The police flew into action and cleared the slogan shouters in ten minutes. The shouting had nothing to do with films. The workers of Devika Rani's estate had a number of grievances, and their immediate bosses had done nothing about them and were just milking the lady's wealth and reputation. Or so it was said. In sheer desperation, the workers had planned for a spectacular demonstration during what they thought was an important public occasion. It is doubtful whether she even understood the situation. They said her last public appearance was in 1970 when she was awarded the Dadasaheb Phalke Award.

The function began. The director of the film festival welcomed Devika Rani and invited her to say a few words and inaugurate the festival.

Devika Rani began her speech with a homage to all the pioneers of cinema. Oratory wasn't her cup of tea. After a few sentences, she suddenly remembered John Ford whose retrospective had been planned as part of the festival. 'What a great artist he is! He has created some wonderful films. I am so excited he is coming to the festival. Is he here?'

The director of the festival intervened with a perfectly audible whisper, 'Mr Ford isn't coming. We are only showing his films.' Devika Rani was annoyed. 'Why didn't you people tell me before?' she asked into the microphone. She added, 'People who organize these festivals should pay some attention to their guests.' It just wasn't her day.

Devika Rani came out of the hall after her speech. Outside, there was a chaotic gathering of guests and onlookers. The cinema hall, Kapali, was situated on a narrow thoroughfare and her car couldn't reach her unhindered. I had also got out of the hall and saw Devika Rani looking lost. I didn't want to add to her discomfiture but when you come face-to-face with a person you thought you knew, there had to be a reaction. I smiled weakly and said, 'You spoke well.' 'Did I?' she asked. Just then her driver had succeeded in getting the vehicle to her and she got in and the car moved. She waved her hand to me more out of habit. I was sure she didn't remember seeing me fifteen years ago.

Fifteen years is a long time. In the year 1964, Gemini Studios was releasing its latest film *Zindagi*. Normally, the Boss and a few technicians would go to three cities—Calcutta, Bombay and Delhi—for the release of Hindi films but the cost-cutting in 1964 allowed only a group of second-line technicians to attend the premiere in Bangalore.

Ten of us went in a Fiat and a Chevrolet station wagon. I do not know whose brainwave it was, but we all landed at Devika Rani's place one afternoon. The place looked like a jungle. The bungalow was an old, low-roofed colonial structure—broad verandas all around the main bungalow. The drawing room was somewhat dark mainly because of a surfeit of furniture and flowerpots. There were at least three French tables leaning against the walls on oddly placed pairs of legs.

Devika Rani welcomed us and we sat on anything that could support a human being. Our sound engineer brother worked for Mr Mehboob in Bombay and this important piece of information was conveyed to our host. Then silence. Silence. More silence.

Just then someone brought us tea. 'Do you expect any song in your new film to become a hit?' Devika Rani asked. We gave her a jumble of contradictory answers. Actually, the premiere had not been a stirring one. The film did run well later in a few places but the first show wasn't very encouraging. 'Even in those days it was difficult to say which was the real draw—

the film or the music. But if a film ran well, the songs became hits even when they were sung by non-singers. For example . . .' she paused to remember. She was approaching sixty but things were obviously slowing down. 'For example . . . for example . . .' she struggled.

'*Chal chal re naujawan*,' I said. That was the song from the Bombay Talkies' 1940 hit *Bandhan* sung by the actor Ashok Kumar; it became a kind of national anthem by popular choice. Devika Rani headed Bombay Talkies at one time.

Suddenly the air turned electric. Devika Rani exploded with vivacity. She had so many things to talk about—Zohrabai, Saigal, Pankaj Mullick, K.C. Dey. Even music directors—Anil Biswas, Khemchand Prakash, Saraswati Devi. Saraswati Devi was the one who composed the tunes for *Chal chal re naujawan*. Devika Rani made a striking observation: all Hindi film music was either Punjabi or Bengali.

My colleagues had become terribly restless. Here was a case of two people isolating a crowd of ten. The senior-most member of the group, an art director, got up, saying, 'We must be in time for the afternoon show.'

Actually, the cinema hall was a most inhospitable place for us. The film had opened in a lukewarm manner and the staff of the cinema hall was cold to us. They made us linger in the foyer or the open corridors leading to the toilets.

Then we trooped out of the house, led by the art director. Devika Rani came up to the portico to see us off.

Suddenly she said, 'One minute', and plucked a flower from a plant nearest to her. With infinite charm, she gave the flower to me. Sadly, the flower dropped off the stem as we were getting into the station wagon.

What made Devika Rani entrust herself so totally to the hands of a person who talked of a will even before the funeral had taken place?

Is it possible that the person also knew the song *Chal chal re naujawan*?

13

The Boss in 1966

On 26 February 1966, I completed fourteen years with the Boss. What did those years mean to me? I had under me the largest workforce any other person in the studio had. I had become answerable for their performance and efficiency for the studio's stability and growth. I had married off my younger sister, got my younger brother to marry, lost my mother, and lit the funeral pyre of a number of relations who died without a specific relative entitled to do the last rites. I lost my mother almost exactly as I did my father—she died while I was out to get a specialist who had promised to come at eight but went on with the patients who were at his house. 'Just this person, the very last,' he would say. When at last he came with me in a car I had specially arranged for his visit, my mother had died. That was in 1964.

Vasan's magnum opus *Raj Tilak* hadn't done well at all. Neither Vyjayanthimala nor C. Ramachandra could salvage the film. Vasan must have told himself no more cloak-and-dagger films. The result was *Zindagi* with a lot of star power and an interesting story. Shankar–Jaikishan's music was used for the first time in a Gemini film. Then came *Grihasti*, a film with Ashok Kumar. It had a Tamil version with Sivaji Ganesan in it. This film ran into censor trouble. There was a scene of a mock parliament of children discussing a parent's integrity. The censor board objected to children sitting in judgement over parents. Then came co-productions with Ramanand Sagar. *Ghunghat* was Tagore's novel *Wreck* but Sagar's film followed a very successful Telugu film version of the novel. By this time, Vasan's son-in-law and son began to make their presence felt. A number of old-timers were abruptly asked to leave and that included an expert cameraman and an exceptional sound recorder. But the biggest amputation was C.E. Biggs, head not only of the sound department but also a kind of maintenance engineer of all the equipment of the studio. The lab chief was sent away for being rude to a customer, and a similar case of behaviour was the undoing of a small fry in the editing department. R.K. Narayan's brother, R.K. Ramachandran, also of the editing department, was asked to go. This proved to be a blessing to him because he would go on to join the faculty of the Film Institute of India at Poona and finally retire as the censor officer, a Central government gazetted position. But an equally accomplished N.V. Ramanarasan with his MA in maths and creator of four plays couldn't find the right job easily. He worked for CARE, an NGO, and then another. Suddenly he fell ill and went into a coma. He was a man who practised yoga, could meditate for an hour at a stretch, and he falls into coma! He was in a hospital for about two weeks and passed away without knowing he was dying. The irony is that he was chosen by Vasan personally just as I was chosen.

My position was far from a happy one. True, I had a carpeted room with a telephone extension all for myself. It was a convenient place for a number of people to make phone calls with a certain degree of privacy. But my work space was at the reception counter which was also the place where I had to organize the studio's transport function, oversee the ever-absent conservancy staff, man a petrol pump, and keep accounts of not only the studio's cars but also see that the pump's tank did not go dry. There was quite a lot of confusion in the conversion of gallons to litres. It is approximately 4.5 litres to a gallon, not too complicated to me but was so to everyone who was entitled to the pump—Vasan's personal car, his son's and son-in-law's cars, son-in-law's truck, etc.

Vasan's son and son-in-law were comparatively new to management, much less to be in charge of the variegated staff of Gemini Studios who worked more out of their love and devotion to the Boss rather than monetary considerations. Any film, even the stupidest, needed careful making and assembling which did not conform to calendar and clock. The people engaged at work at a particular time had to be free of distraction, both material and personal. Vasan managed it instinctively and even when he dispensed with a person, the person never bore a grudge against the Boss. People who worked in Gemini Studios never could accept any other person or an organization as an alternative to the Boss. They suffered—but never cursed. Such was the emotional bond Vasan elicited from his men.

Even infrastructure aspects showed wrong judgement. For a while, in India, there was a colour system called Gevacolor. Though a few Hollywood films did use this system, it was soon abandoned and Eastman Color became the absolute champion. But Gemini Studios went for Gevacolor, the standardization of which cost millions and a number of years. The result was loss of goodwill, time and a considerable amount of money. Finally, Gemini had to go with Eastman Color.

In my case, human relations became the bone of contention, the transport department, to name one. Gemini Studios had three passenger cars and a Chevrolet ten-seater. Eight drivers and two cleaners. Split them into two— four drivers and a cleaner for each shift of eight hours. During shooting days, this workforce was totally inadequate. So the studio hired a freelance driver and sometimes engaged 'private taxis'. Not strictly legal but that was how film units functioned. The government departments were lenient because films then still ignited a certain juvenile excitement. When we had casual drivers and 'private taxis', the regular drivers would want all the difficult trips to be given to the PTs. The taxi drivers would obey without a whimper but they would not know all the men and women needed for a particular schedule. The regular drivers would know and so, invariably, they had the most trips. Dropping people home was all that the casual vehicles and drivers could manage. A not-so-practical union leader had drawn up drivers' rights and obligations. A driver's shift had to be eight hours with one-hour break for lunch. As though to compensate for this hour, they could claim overtime wages only after being on duty for nine hours! Even this piece of injustice, the drivers did not mind. When it came to getting food for actors and the shooting staff, money was thrown about without any concern, while the management would not grant lunch allowance for drivers. It was a pittance—ten annas. A little more than half a rupee. And I had to be the demon to implement these slices of pettiness.

Naturally, there was friction and all round unhappiness. I bore it all up to a point. Then I sought a meeting with the Boss. The Boss said, 'You must have a complaint upon which I can take action. No use saying disobedience of drivers.'

I would be the last person to let a miserable driver face an inquiry. I said, 'I can't name an individual. My complaint is against the system.'

'A system well established can't be changed just like that.'

But in two months' time, I was again before him. 'Any complaint?' he asked.

'It is a complaint against me. I am a writer. I have been published all over India and once or twice abroad too. I can't be enforcing discipline among drivers and the conservancy staff.'

'Can you show me anything you have published?'

I showed him a number of Tamil and English journals and papers.

He looked at them. A moment of unending silence.

'If you were a writer, you wouldn't have been doing all these things for so many years.'

I was dumbfounded. Again, the fault was mine and he had scored over me hands down. Why have I been available to be entrusted with a myriad trifles?

I didn't sleep that night. I thought over what he said. Finally, on 6 June 1966, I went to see him. I found his son in his seat. I don't think he had the slightest inkling of what had taken place between me and the Boss during the last few months. I told the son, 'I am resigning.'

'I see. Have you brought your resignation letter?'

'I have.'

'You are relieved straightaway. You have any office cash to hand over?'

'No. Can I see the Boss?'

'Boss may not come to office for a few days.'

So I left the Boss and his studio in an anticlimactic manner.

Fourteen years! That was the period Rama was to spend in banishment. It was also the period—more or less—the Pandava princes were in exile.

In 1967, the Boss sent for me to help a labour leader take out a souvenir. The Congress was in the process of splitting. The special publication was from the Indira Gandhi faction. The one abuse they hurled at Kamaraj was bossism! All the articles were against bosses and bossism!

I got it done in a week's time. Months later, I met the labour leader and asked him, 'Did you notice the pages in the souvenir were jumbled?'

'No. Is it?'

'Didn't anyone tell you?'

'No.'

But I was sure the bosses would have noticed and had a good laugh. The splinter group could not even abuse them correctly. And they wanted to rule the country! But rule they did.

*

But the Boss had kept a secret even from his family. Three years after I left Gemini Studios, he died of cancer. No one knew he was dying. I went to Gemini House and there he was laid on the floor, north to south. My father's friend. He remembered my father, even in the days I worked for him. I felt so sad. He looked sad too. He seemed to say, 'Sorry, son. Shouldn't have dragged you here from Secunderabad.'

Afterword

Though the Boss died in 1969, the Gemini Studios continued to make films for a few more years until a trilingual disaster in 1975 closed it down. Ironically, the title of the film was *All People Are Good*.

With the Boss still around, there were some hits though not as thundering as *Chandralekha* and *Sansar*. Sagar Arts, in association with Gemini Studios, made a hit with *Ghunghat*. *Grihasti*, directed by Kishore Sahu, in an Indian sense, had a fairly original story and it won a prestigious all-India award for a song. Another big hit was *Gharana*, a Hindi version of a Telugu film based on a Tamil play by the veteran B.S. Ramaiah.

The Boss planned to make a remake of a Tamil film, *Chiththi*, meaning stepmother. Even in Tamil, it was a loud film, with all the possible situations when a young woman in a traditional Hindu family is forced to marry an elderly widower, forsaking her own preferences. When the remake was decided upon, everyone thought Meena Kumari was the right person to play the main role. But she had too many of her own problems. Ultimately, the film was done with a more dependable South Indian star—Padmini. Then there were remakes of a Malayalam film titled *Thulabharam* and K. Balachander's Tamil hit *Bama Vijayam*. The Tamil film hinged on the story of a thin incident of a film star promising to visit the home of a joint family of three married brothers. Hence, the Hindi title *Teen Bahuranian*. The irony was that the wives were even more interested in making an impression on the star—a pretty woman, of course. The three sons have an elderly father always issuing warning that spendthrifts end up in a mess.

That semi-comical, semi-didactic character was played in Hindi by Prithviraj Kapoor who had earlier delivered authoritarian lines in *Mughale-Azam* and *Rustom Sohrab*. The Boss was alive for *Teen Bahuranian*. He watched the film. Prithviraj's lines were unintelligible. The great actor's voice wasn't at its best! Now, only the Boss could set the problem right. He called up the actor with the once-stentorian voice and told him that he had not done justice to himself in dialogue delivery, and asked him whether he could use a dubbed voice. Prithviraj was more than happy. He must have had misgivings himself and now with a proper professional voice, his role would come off even better. It certainly did. It was a problem which only a man of Vasan's stature could solve and he did it with exemplary directness and grace. I thought he displayed the same grace when he sent for to me to edit an anti-bossism souvenir being brought out by rebel Congressmen. He might even have been sorry that I resigned when he was not present. All he would have done was ask me to wait a little more.

All this is now an old story. Fifty years is a long time.

Chennai,   Ashokamitran
2015